Cyber Warfare

Prepping for Tomorrow Series

A Preparedness Guide by

Bobby Akart

&

The Staff of Freedom Preppers

First edition.

Copyright Information

DEDICATIONS

To the love of my life, you saved me from madness
and continue to do so daily.

To the Princesses of the Palace, my little marauders in training,
you have no idea how much happiness you bring
to your Mommy and me.

To my fellow preppers;
never be ashamed of adopting a preparedness lifestyle.

ACKNOWLEDGEMENTS

For their efforts in making The Boston Brahmin series a reality,
I would like to thank Hristo Argirov Kovatliev for his incredible
cover art, Pauline Nolet for her editorial prowess, Stef Mcdaid for
making this manuscript readable on so many formats, and The
Team—whose advice, friendship and attention to detail is priceless.

Thank you!!

ABOUT THE AUTHOR

Author of two Amazon #1 Bestsellers for both fiction (*Evil, Meet Opportunity*—Action, Adventure category) and nonfiction (*Seeds of Liberty*—Politics, Social Sciences and Modern History categories), Bobby Akart has provided his readers a diverse range of topics that are both informative and entertaining.

Born and raised in Tennessee, Bobby received his bachelor's degree with a dual major in Economics and Political Science. He not only understands how the economy works, but the profound effect politics has on the economy as well. After completing his undergraduate degree at Tennessee in three years, he entered the dual-degree program, obtaining a Juris Doctor combined with an MBA—Master of Business Administration at the age of twenty-three.

His education perfectly suited him for his legal career in banking, trusts and investment banking. As his legal career flourished, business opportunities arose, including the operation of restaurants and the development of commercial real estate. But after meeting and marrying the love of his life, they left the corporate world and developed online businesses.

A life-changing event led them to Muddy Pond, Tennessee where he and his wife lead a self-sustainable, preparedness lifestyle. Bobby and his wife are unabashed preppers and share their expert knowledge of prepping via their website www.FreedomPreppers.com.

Bobby lives in the back woods of the Cumberland Plateau with his wife and fellow author, Danni Elle, their two English bulldogs, aka the Princesses of the Palace, a variety of farm animals, thirteen Pekin ducks and a herd of a dozen bunnies, and counting.

You can contact Bobby directly by email (BobbyAkart@gmail.com) or through his website www.BobbyAkart.com

FOREWORD BY STEVEN KONKOLY

Where to start? Bobby Akart has been a tireless proponent of prepper fiction writers, going far above and beyond the call of duty to support and promote authors. From the very first time I spoke with Bobby, I was impressed with his positive attitude and willingness to share. It's the kind of selflessness that makes you wonder *what's the catch*? Well, there is no catch! Bobby is just a stand-up guy—with many talents.

I was familiar with Bobby's writing via the American Preppers Network and his website—FreedomPreppers.com. I wanted to get Bobby out of the shadows and into the limelight, so I suggested Bobby try writing fiction. His addition to my Perseid Collapse Kindle World reached an Amazon #1 Bestseller ranking in the Kindle Worlds Action and Adventure category. From that point forward, Bobby was hooked, and a new author was born.

In addition to the very successful Boston Brahmin series, Bobby wrote a nonfiction companion guide to the series—Seeds of Liberty. Also, an Amazon #1 Bestseller in the Politics, Social Sciences, and History categories, Seeds of Liberty exhibits Bobby's versatility in writing both fiction and nonfiction works.

In The Boston Brahmin series, political suspense collides with post-apocalyptic thriller fiction. Bobby's attention to detail and real-world scenarios immerses the reader in a world of geopolitical machinations and post-apocalyptic drama.

The Prepping for Tomorrow series is the culmination of Bobby's research and real-world experiences provided in a concise guide for new and experienced preppers alike. Author Bobby Akart possesses the analytic capability of a supercomputer coupled with the expressiveness of an exceptional writer. Cyber Warfare is eye-opening.

EPIGRAPH

There are risks and costs to action. But they are far less than the long
range risks of comfortable inaction.
~ John F. Kennedy

I know not with what weapons World War III will be fought, but
World War IV will be fought with sticks and stones.
~Albert Einstein

Civilization is like a thin layer of ice upon a deep ocean
of chaos and darkness.
~ Werner Herzog

Timeo Danaos et dona ferentis ~ Beware of Greeks bearing gifts.
~ Vergil's words for the voice of Laocoon in the Aeneid

By failing to prepare, you are preparing to fail.
~ Benjamin Franklin

In war, knowledge must become capability.
~ Carl von Clausewitz, *On War*

The End Of The World As We Know It
TEOTWAWKI

Contents

ABOUT CYBER WARFARE AND THE PREPPING FOR TOMORROW SERIES

Because you never know when the day before —
is the day before.
Prepare for tomorrow!

What if the preppers are right?

The media shapes public opinion in all formats including news, cinema and television shows. It should come as no surprise that everyone doesn't necessarily form an opinion on every subject. Nor should you be shocked to hear that most opinions are uninformed. We can all give countless examples of this. Most Americans are *sheeple*, unable to think for themselves. They are content to follow, and many are too lazy to do the minimal research required to have an informed opinion. Their reliance on government or media sources for information makes them susceptible to manipulation. It's simply easier to be a *sheeple*.

As a student of the preparedness lifestyle, I cringe at the media's portrayal of preppers. Initially, the brunt of the ridicule was directed at survivalists. But with the success of National Geographic's Doomsday Preppers, the concept of being a prepper hit the mainstream. Now Preppers are the target of the media's derision. I have my opinion as to why that is the case, and it has its basis in politics. It is my opinion that the media is largely left-leaning and, as a result, does not embrace the self-sufficient lifestyle that is prepping. So, if you can't join them, beat them down—repeatedly. As a recent example, consider the media's dismantling of the Tea Party movement. I see similar attacks on preppers.

From the Associated Press: "*Sandy Hook Shooter Comes from Prepper Family.*"

From CBS: "*Local 'Preppers' Stock Up For Improbable US Ebola Crisis.*"

From Washington Post: "*'Preppers' Convinced Yellowstone Volcano Spells Doom.*"

But, what if the Preppers are right?

What if?

The Economy Collapses

The United States economy can collapse as a result of our own government's mismanagement of our national debt or external factors such as a global financial meltdown, an attack on the US Dollar, and other *predictable* events. Why do you think the Federal Reserve is so frightened of raising interest rates despite apparent underlying inflation data? Our economy is a house of cards. We are just a few steps away from a collapse of the dollar and hyperinflation.

History is replete with the rise and fall of empires. Are Americans so arrogant, or oblivious, to realize that we are in a stage of decline and collapse? Some of the signs of decline include a downward cultural spiral, an over-reliance on government and the inability to protect the integrity of a nation's borders. Sound familiar? **All empires collapse eventually. There have been no exceptions in the history of humanity.**

None. All empires end when a more vigorous empire defeats them—or when their financing runs out.

What if?

Escalation of Global Conflict into a World War

Let's compile a list of the strongest, most dangerous *bad actors* on the world geopolitical stage:

Russia ~ China ~ North Korea ~ Iran ~ Syria ~ ISIS ~ Al Qaeda

What do these seven geopolitical foes have in common? They both hate and disrespect the United States! Think of the Seven Deadly Sins: Lust, Gluttony, Greed, Sloth, Wrath, Envy, Pride. All of these relate to the attitudes of these *bad actors* towards the United States. Is it that far fetched that one or more of these could band together to bring the mighty United States of America to it's knees? Remember the words of the great Chinese General Sun Tzu — *the enemy of my enemy is my friend.* Except ISIS and Al Qaeda, the five nations comprising this group considers each other allies.

The assassination of an Archduke precipitated World War I, but the underlying causes were geopolitical tensions in Europe. 20 million people died during the war followed by another 70 million post-war due to famine and the Spanish Flu. Are we naive to think that something like this couldn't happen again? *Geopolitical tensions* - sound familiar?

Tensions arising from invasions of other sovereign territories around the world was the principal cause of World War II. It escalated into a global conflict with the Japanese attack on Pearl Harbor. Today, Russia has invaded Ukraine. China prepares to exert more of its dominance in Asia. ISIS is taking over large parts of the Middle East to form an Islamic State. Some might say— *not our problem.* But what if one of the *bad actors* mentioned above decide to make it our problem with an attack on the heartland along the lines of Pearl Harbor? Is that so far fetched? Remember 9/11?

What if?

America is Attacked

We are vulnerable to attack because of our desire to provide freedoms to all Americans, but especially because of political correctness. We are not allowed to use racial profiling to identify a potential terrorist. Our southern border is a sieve. We refuse to ban flights from Ebola-stricken countries for fear of being labeled racist. Our military has been weakened by prolonged wars and budget cuts.

Our enemies can come at us in so many ways. A day does not go by without news of a cyber-terrorism incident. What if these cyber attacks are just a series of trial runs before one large massive, coordinated attack on our banking, governmental and utility servers? An electromagnetic pulse delivered by a nuclear warhead or a series of electromagnetic pulse weapons fired at strategic locations across the country could bring down our power grid. For the first time, Russia has more deployed nuclear assets than the United States does. Can you say "outnumbered"?

What if?

Widespread Pandemic or BioTerror

Our government is intent on *calming the fears* of the American people as to the likelihood of the Ebola virus hitting US soil. The presence of the Ebola virus came as a result of bringing Ebola-stricken health care workers into the country. Keep in mind that these were people who are experts in treating this virus and who were provided all of the necessary equipment to prevent contracting Ebola. As the CDC was calming our fears, a Nigerian national flew into Dallas with Ebola potentially infecting hundreds and ultimately dying while in the government's care.

The question has to be asked—*What is wrong with a little fear amongst the masses?*

Fear is a great motivator; it is designed to be compelling so that we take survival action in the form of fight, flight, or freeze.

In 1763, the British fortress at Fort Pitt in Delaware was under siege. Letters were exchanged between British General Jeffrey

Amherst and Colonel Henry Bouquet as to proposed defensive tactics.

General Amherst suggested: *"Could it not be contrived to send the Smallpox among those disaffected tribes of Indians?"*

Weaponized smallpox. Is it not plausible that our enemies could weaponize Ebola? In the name of Jihad, is it not possible that one would contract the Ebola virus and enter the United States with the intention of creating a pandemic? The news outlets that raise these possibilities are labeled fear mongers and racists. But have you noticed that Amazon is selling out of particulate masks and other bio-hazard supplies? Fear is a great motivator.

What if?

Near Earth Object - SuperVolcano Eruption - Natural Disaster

Any of the above naturally occurring events could wreak havoc on our power grid, our atmosphere, and our climate. These are not the catastrophic events known only in science fiction movies. There is a historical precedent for them all.

A major earthquake along the New Madrid Fault in the central United States could collapse bridges over the Mississippi River. An earthquake of this magnitude along the New Madrid happened before in 1811 and 1812. The New Madrid Seismic Zone (NMSZ) is comprised of eight states: Alabama, Arkansas, Illinois, Indiana, Kentucky, Mississippi, Missouri, and Tennessee.

The Wabash Valley Seismic Zone (WVSZ) in southern Illinois and southeast Indiana together with the East Tennessee Seismic Zone in eastern Tennessee and northeastern Alabama, constitute a significant risk of moderate-to-severe earthquakes throughout the central region of the USA.

Studies indicate the Tennessee will incur the highest level of economic damage and societal impact. According to the Mid-America Earthquake Center, over 300,000 buildings would be moderately or more severely damaged, over 290,000 people will be displaced and well over 70,000 casualties are expected. Total direct economic losses surpass $56 billion. These results focus on the immediate effects of the massive earthquake itself. As preppers, we consider the ancillary impact in the form of societal unrest — looting, death from sickness and murder.

The States of Missouri, Arkansas, Kentucky and Illinois would also incur significant losses. Studies indicate a potential direct economic loss reaching over $150 billion.

The indirect economic loss due to business interruption and loss of market share is at least as high if not far greater than the direct economic losses. Scientists and economists predict the total economic impact of a series of NMSZ earthquakes is likely to constitute the highest economic loss due to a natural disaster in U.S. history.

The economic losses and societal impact for each state should be considered separately. Since each scenario is based on a different hazard, adding results together will not reflect an accurate scenario. It 's hard to gauge the potential loss of life resulting from a natural disaster of this magnitude.

Critical infrastructure and lifelines will also be heavily damaged and will be out of service after the earthquake for a considerable period. The resulting collapse of the power grid and transportation routes are likely to affect a region much larger than the eight states referenced above. Many hospitals nearest to the epicenter will not be able to care for its patients. Many of those injured during the disaster will have to be transported outside of the region for medical attention. Moreover, pre-disaster patients will be required to continue their care outside of the area to fully functioning hospitals.

It is doubtful that the transportation system will be intact. Damage to the transportation system will hinder mass evacuation efforts. First responders will be severely impaired due to police and fire stations throughout the impacted region. Public shelters will be damaged and unusable after the earthquake.

The scenario described for a New Madrid Zone earthquake can be applied to other catastrophic disaster events. Strikes by near earth objects such as asteroids can be extinction level events. Likewise, a massive eruption of the Yellowstone Super Volcano could result in climate change that would alter the entire food production system of the Northern Hemisphere.

What if?

Coronal Mass Ejection – Solar Flare

Imagine our way of life without power for weeks on end as a result of a massive solar flare striking the Earth. It happened in 1859 in what is commonly referred to as the Carrington Event.

For telegraph operators in the Americas and Europe, however, the experience caused chaos. Many found that their lines were just unusable—they could neither send nor receive messages. Others were able to operate even with their power supplies turned off, using only the current in the air from the solar storm.

From historical reports, one telegraph operator said "The line was in perfect order, and skilled operators worked incessantly from eight o'clock last evening until one o'clock this morning to transmit, in an intelligible form, four hundred words of the report per steamer Indian for the Associated Press."

Other operators experienced physical danger. Washington, D.C., operator Frank Royce said "I received a very severe electric shock, which stunned me for an instant. An old man who was sitting facing me, and but a few feet distant, said that he saw a spark of fire jump from my forehead to the sounder."

At the time, the telegraph was a new technology and never experienced technical difficulties of this type. But the story offers an important warning for modern society. The Carrington Event, as the 1859 solar storm has been named, provides evidence of the fragility of electrical infrastructure. Scientific American reported in October of 1859: "The electromagnetic basis of the various phenomena was identified relatively quickly. A connection between the northern lights and forces of electricity and magnetism is now fully established."

Over the last one hundred and fifty years, the world's critical infrastructure has become a more integral part of daily life. In the nineteenth century, telegraphs composed a comparatively small and relatively non-essential part of everyday life. Their successors today—including the electrical grid and much of the telecommunications network—are essential to modern life.

Is the current system any more protected from catastrophic interference than the telegraph of the nineteenth century? Can the power grid handle a terrorist attack, or severe weather events, or a solar storm?

There's never been a real test to prove it, but there is a robust debate about the vulnerability of the power grid. The most dangerous and costly possibilities for major catastrophes, the collapse of the nation's critical infrastructure, might visit the United States from any number of methods.

One scenario is a repeat of the solar storm as big as the 1859 Carrington. A solar event of this magnitude hasn't struck the earth since, although there have been smaller ones. In 1989, a coronal mass ejection caused a blackout across parts of Canada, especially in Quebec. As a result of complications across the interconnected grid, a large transformer in New Jersey permanently failed.

In 2003, residents of the northeastern United States experienced a grid down scenario. It doesn't take an unprecedented solar flare to knock out power. The combination of a few trees touching power lines, and a few power companies asleep at the wheel, plunged a section of the nation into darkness. The darkness can spread. As the difficulties at Ohio-based FirstEnergy grew and eventually cascaded over the grid, electrical service from Detroit to New York City was lost. The 2003 event was a comparatively minor episode compared to what might have happened. Most customers had their power back within a couple of days, and the transformers were relatively unaffected.

Compare this event with the incident in Auckland, New Zealand. Cables supplying power to the downtown business district failed in 1998. The center of the city went dark. Companies were forced to shutter or relocate their operations outside the affected area. The local Auckland utility had to adopt drastic measures to move in temporary generators. They even enlisted the assistance of the world's largest cargo plane—owned by rock band *U2*, to transport massive generators into the area. It took five weeks for the power grid to be fully restored.

There are contrarians. Jeff Dagle, an electrical engineer at the Pacific Northwest National Laboratory who served on the Northeast Blackout Investigation Task Force argues "one lesson of the 2003 blackout is that the power grid is more resilient than you might think."

The task force investigators pinpointed four separate root causes for the collapse, and human error played a significant role. "It took an hour for it to collapse with no one managing it," Dagle said. "They would have been just as effective if they had just gone home for the day. That to me just underscores how remarkably stable things are."

As awareness was raised by Congress, the National Academies of Science produced a report detailing the risk of a major solar event. The 2008 NAS report paints a dire picture based on a study conducted for FEMA and Electromagnetic Pulse Commission created by Congress.

While severe solar storms do not occur that often, they have the potential for long-term catastrophic impacts to the nation's power grid. Impacts would be felt on interdependent infrastructures. For example, the potable water distribution will be affected immediately. Pumps and purification facilities rely on electricity. The nation's food supply will be disrupted and most perishable foods will spoil and lost within twenty-four hours. There will be immediate or eventual loss of heating/air conditioning, sewage disposal, phone service, transportation, fuel resupply, and many of the necessities we take for granted.

According to the EMP Commission, the effects will be felt for years, and its economic costs could add up to trillions of dollars—dwarfing the cost of Hurricane Katrina. More importantly, the commission's findings state a potential loss of life that is staggering. Within one year, according to their conclusions, ninety percent of Americans would die.

But skeptics say it's the opposite. Jon Wellinghoff, who served as chairman of the Federal Energy Regulatory Commission—commonly known as FERC, from 2009 to 2013, has sounded the alarm about the danger of an attack on the system. The heightened awareness came as a result of an April 2013 incident in Silicon Valley, California in which a group of attackers conducted a coordinated assault on an electrical substation, knocking out 27 transformers. FERC points to the fact that the U.S. power grid is broken into three big sections known as *interconnections.* There is one each for the Eastern United States, the West, and—out on its own—Texas. In fact, the East and West interconnections also include much of Canada and parts of Mexico.

In a 2013 report, FERC concluded that if a limited number of substations in each of those interconnects were disabled, utilities cannot bring the interconnect back up again for an indeterminate amount of time. FERC's conclusion isn't classified information. This information has been in government reports and widely disseminated on the internet for years.

FERC also notes it could take far longer to return the electrical grid to full functionality than it did in 2003. Wellinghoff said, "If you destroy the transformers—all it takes is one high-caliber bullet through a transformer case, and it's gone, you have to replace it," he said. "If there aren't spares on hand—and in the event of a coordinated attack on multiple substations, any inventory could be exhausted—it takes months to build new ones."

"Once your electricity is out, your gasoline is out, because you can't pump the gas anymore. All your transportation's out, all of your financial transactions are out, of course because there are no electronics," Wellinghoff said.

FERC's proposed solution is to break the system into a series of *microgrids.* In the event of a cascading failure, smaller portions of the countries can isolate themselves from the collapse of the grid. There is a precedent for this. Princeton University has an independent power grid. When a large part of the critical infrastructure collapsed during Superstorm Sandy, the Princeton campus became a place of refuge for residents, and a command center for first responders.

These doomsday scenarios may be beside the point because the electrical grid is already subject to a series of dangerous stresses from climate change. Sandy showed that the assumptions used to build many parts of the electrical grid were wrong. The storm surge overwhelmed the infrastructure, flooding substations and causing them to fail. Significant portions of the grid might need to be moved to higher ground.

Even away from the coasts, extreme weather can threaten the system in unexpected ways. Some systems use gas insulation, but if the temperature drops low enough, the gas composition changes and the insulation fails. Power plants in warmer places like Texas aren't well-prepared for extreme cold, meaning plants could fail when the population most needs them to provide power for heat. As utilities rely more heavily on natural gas to generate power, there's a danger of demand exceeding supply. A likely scenario is a blizzard in which everyone cranks up their propane or natural gas-powered heating systems. As the system becomes overwhelmed, the gas company can't provide to everyone. Power providers don't necessarily have the first right of refusal from their sources, so they could lose supplies and be forced to power down in the middle of a winter storm.

Summer doesn't offer any respite. Even prolonged droughts play a role. As consumers turn up their air conditioners, requests for more power increased. There can be a ratcheting effect. If there are several days of consistently high temperatures, buildings never cool completely. The demand from local utilities will peak higher and higher each day. Power plants rely upon groundwater to cool their systems. They will struggle to maintain cooling as the water itself heats up. Droughts can diminish the power from hydroelectric plants, especially in the western United States.

If extreme weather continues to be the norm, the chaos unleashed on the grid by Sandy may be just a preview of the sorts of disruptions to the grid that might become commonplace. Or as the New York Herald argued in 1859, referring to the Carrington event, "Phenomena are not supposed to have any reference to things past—

only to things to come. Therefore, the aurora borealis must be connected with something in the future—war, or pestilence, or famine." Although the impact of solar storms was not fully understood at the time, the prediction of catastrophe remains valid.

Science Fiction or Reality

All of the events described above are plausible and have their roots in history. What could happen? Global Panic. Martial Law. Travel Restrictions. Food and Water Shortages. An Overload of the Medical System. Societal Collapse. Economic Collapse.

This is why we prep. Prepping is insurance against both natural and man-made catastrophic events. The government now requires you to carry medical insurance. Your homeowner's insurance may include damage from tornadoes. Even though you may never incur damage from a tornado, you pay for that coverage monthly nonetheless. This is what preppers do. We allocate time and resources to protect our families in the event of seemingly unlikely events but events that are occurring daily or have historical precedent.

At Freedom Preppers, we hope none of these catastrophic events occur, but *what if*?

CYBER ATTACK

Simply put, a Cyber Attack is a deliberate exploitation of computer systems. Cyber Attacks are used to gain access to information but can also be used to alter computer code, insert malware or take over the operations of a computer driven network.

Why would terrorists bother with an elaborate, dangerous physical operation—complete with all the recon and planning of a black ops mission—when they could achieve the same effect from the comfort of their home? An effective cyber attack could, if cleverly designed, produce a great deal of physical damage very quickly, and interconnections in digital operations would mean such an attack could bypass fail safes in the physical infrastructure that stop cascading failures.

One string of 1s and 0s could have a significant impact. If a computer hacker could command all the circuit breakers in a utility to open, the system will be overloaded. Power utility personnel sitting in the control room could do it. A proficient cyber-terrorist can do it as well. In fact, smart-grid technologies are more susceptible to common computer failures. New features added to make the system easily manageable might render it more vulnerable.

At least one major public official downplays the cyber attack scenario. The nation's top disaster responder, FEMA director Craig Fugate, shrugs at the threat of an power grid collapse.

"When have people panicked? Generally what you find is the birth rate goes up nine months later," he said, then turned more serious: "People are much more resilient than the professionals would give them credit for. Would it be unpleasant? Yes. Would it be uncomfortable? Have you ever seen the power go out, and traffic signals stop working? Traffic's hell but people figure it out."

Fugate's big worry in a mass outage is communication, he said. When people can get information and know how long power will be out, they handle it much better.

Don't worry, the government will take care of you. Naïve.

In poll after poll, one of the threats concerning preppers is the use of a cyber attack to cause a grid down scenario. There are many bad actors on the international stage. Each is capable of wreaking havoc in the US by shutting down our power grid and enjoying the resulting chaos.

No bombs. No bullets. No swordfights. Just a few keystrokes on the computer. And we're done.

Cyber Warfare is a primer on the threats we face as a nation from the *bad actors* mentioned above. This guide will also help you answer the question:

What if?

PART ONE

WHAT IS CYBER WARFARE?

CHAPTER ONE
CYBER TERMINOLOGY

What is cyber warfare?

Every media outlet or talk show uses the terms *cyber warfare*, *cyber terrorism*, and *cyber vandalism*, often in dire and apocalyptic tones. Reports may depict some obscure but imminent danger or threat to our nation, our corporate enterprises, or even our personal liberties. Visit a technological vendor expo or a security conference and you will hear the same terms in the same tones. Knowing that fear is a great motivator, the vendors use the terms to frighten you into believing your information is unsafe unless you purchase the numerous products or services available to combat the *cyber-whatever*.

As you follow news reports or conduct your research on the subject, you will not find clear and standardized definitions of what constitutes *cyber warfare*, *cyber terrorism*, *cyber espionage* and *cyber vandalism*. Many resources can't even agree on the spelling. Is *cyber warfare* one word or two? Should a dash connect them?

Because of this, it's become increasingly difficult to cut through the hyperbole and truly understand the risk associated with the technological advances the human race has achieved. For example, depending on perspective, some politicians and pundits believe the United States is engaged in cyber warfare with North Korea. But on the other hand, President Obama dismissed the Sony hack as cyber vandalism. Who's right? It depends on one's perspective or agenda.

The issue of definition is exacerbated by the fact such terms are often used interchangeably and without regard to the corresponding real-world equivalents. The first step in the analysis of Cyber Warfare is to find and provide a common language to help wade through the politicking and marketing.

Our planet will always be in a state of constant conflict. Our technological advances reach from the physical realm into the network of interconnected telecommunications equipment known as cyberspace. Private-sector firms, government institutions, the military, criminals, terrorists, and spies are all actors in the theater of cyberspace. Each of these actors may have varying goals that are all interwoven, operating within the same medium. What separates these actors and accounts for the different definitions in *cyber* terms are their ideologies, objectives, and methods.

The best way to forge an understanding of the differences in terms is to look at the conventional definitions of certain words and directly apply them to cyberspace. For example, traditional, kinetic warfare has a precise definition that 's hard to dispute—*a conflict between two or more governments or militaries that include death, property destruction and collateral damage as an objective.* Cyber warfare, therefore, uses the same principles of goals, actors and methods that one can examine against a cyber attack to ascertain the gravity of the situation.

Let's examine two of the most common phrases used, "cyberspace" and "cyber attack" and get to the root of what they mean.

Cyberspace & Cyber Attacks

The realm in which all of this takes place is cyberspace, and as previously stated, can be thought of as a theater of operation.

Author William Gibson coined the term cyberspace in his science fiction hit *Neuromancer*. The novel tells the story of a washed-up computer hacker hired by a mysterious employer to pull off the ultimate hack — enter the mind of a powerful artificial intelligence orbiting the earth. This novel has over a million copies in print.

The Department of Defense defines cyberspace as—*A domain characterized by the use of electronics and the electromagnetic spectrum to store, modify, and exchange data via networked systems and associated physical infrastructures.*

A good analogy to help understand the concept of cyberspace. Let's draw a parallel to your physical space. You, dear reader, are a person, and you are somewhere—perhaps an office, house or by the pool reading this on your Kindle. This is your environment, your space. You have objects around you that you interact with—a spouse, a sofa, a TV, or building. You are an actor in this space, and there are other actors around you; most have good intentions, and some have evil intentions. At any point, someone in this environment can act against you or act against an object in the environment.

Cyberspace is essentially the same: it is an environment in which you operate. Instead of physically *being* somewhere, you are using computer equipment to interact over a network and connect to other resources that give you information. Instead of *objects*, like a car or a sofa, you have email, websites, games, and databases.

Just like real life, most people you interact with are benign, but some are malicious. In the physical space, a vandal can pick up a spray paint can and tag your car. In cyberspace, a vandal can replace your website's home page with web defacement. This is called a cyber attack, and the vandal is a cyber-vandal.

The graphic below illustrates the overall cyberspace environment, threat actors, and possible targets. To help you conceptualize this, think about the same model, but in a physical space.

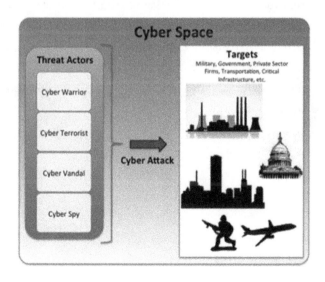

Take away the word *cyber* and you have warriors, terrorists, vandals, and spies that attack a variety of targets. The actual attack may look the same or similar coming from various threat actors, but goals, ideology, and methods differentiate them.

An excellent definition of an attack that occurs in cyberspace comes from James Clapper, Director of National Intelligence—*a non-kinetic offensive operation intended to create physical effects or to manipulate, disrupt, or delete data.* DNI Clapper intentionally left this definition very broad. It does not attempt to attribute political ideologies, motivations, resources, affiliations or objectives. It merely states the characteristics and outcome of the cyber intrusion.

Cyber attacks of varying degrees of destruction occur daily from a variety of actors. Some of the more recent high-profile attacks result from retail data breaches. The Sony Pictures Entertainment hack, website vandalism and distributed denial-of-service (DDoS) attacks are all examples of data breaches.

The groundwork is set for what is a cyberattack and the environment, cyberspace, in which they are launched and experienced by the victim. This is the first step in dispelling myths to understand risk and what is possible—and not possible—when it comes to protecting your firm and the nation.

Now the real fun begins – we'll dissect the four most commonly confused terms: *cyber-terrorism, cyber vandalism, cyber espionage* and *cyber war.* The objective is to dispel myths and, by establishing a shared understanding, provide a way for managers to cut to the chase and understand risk without all the FUD. The graph below shows the four terms and attributes at a glance.

Term	Definition	Perpetrated By	Examples
Cyber War	Attacks in cyber space designed to support a commander's military goals.	Military commanders, government cyber warriors	Russian cyber attacks during the 2008 Russo-Georgian War.
Cyber Terrorism	Religious or politically motivated attacks against non-combatants that cause death, bodily injury and/or serious property damage.	Terrorists, cyber terrorists	None
Cyber Vandalism	Destruction or defacement of public or private property in cyber space.	Cyber Vandals	Website defacement, malware that erases data, distributed denial-of-service (DDoS)
Cyber Espionage	The practice of spying in cyberspace to gain knowledge about a target.	Government-backed intelligence organizations, private sector firms, military	Flame virus, NSA efforts revealed by Snowdèn, Chinese economic espionage

Now let's dig into each definition and examine the fundamentals.

Cyber Terrorism

No one can agree on the appropriate definition of terrorism, and as such, the definition of cyber terrorism is even murkier. Ron Dick, director of the National Infrastructure Protection Center, defines cyber terrorism as a criminal act perpetrated through computers resulting in violence, death, and destruction, and creating terror for the purpose of coercing a government to change its policies.

Many have argued that cyber terrorism does not exist because *cyberspace* is an abstract concept. On the other hand, terror in a shopping mall is a very real, quantifiable event that can lead to bodily harm for the average citizen. Cyber terrorism, as a term, has been used (and misused) so many times to describe a cyber attack, it has almost lost the impact its real world counterpart maintains.

21

According to US Code, Title 22, Chapter 38 § 2656f, terrorism is defined as *premeditated, politically motivated violence perpetrated against non-combatant targets by subnational groups or clandestine agents.*

By definition, a cyber terrorist attack must include violence toward non-combatants and result in large-scale damage or financial harm. Furthermore, it can often be difficult to attribute motivations, goals and affiliations to cyber attacks, which makes attribution and labels difficult in the cases of both accepted acts of terrorism and cyber terrorism.

Based on publically available knowledge, there are no known examples of cyber terrorism. It will happen – it just hasn't happened yet.

Cyber Vandalism

There is not an *official* U.S. government definition of cyber vandalism, although the terminology has been used by the President at times. Supreme Court Justice Potter Stewart opined precise terminology may not be easy to describe, but *you will know it when you see it.*

The traditional definition of *vandalism* from the Merriam-Webster dictionary is the *willful or malicious destruction or defacement of public or private property.*

Cyber vandals usually perpetrate an attack for personal enjoyment or to increase their stature within a group, club or organization. They also act very overtly, wishing to leave a calling card, so the victim and others may assign responsibility. Some conventional methods are website defacement, denial-of-service attacks, forced system outages and data destruction.

Here is an example from the hacktivist group Anonymous.

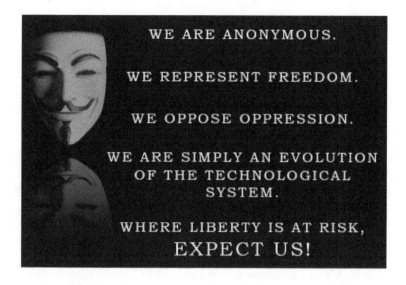

The following are a few examples of cyber vandalism from Wikipedia:

Anonymous DDoS attacks on various targets in 2011-2012

Operation Payback was a coordinated group of attacks on high-profile opponents of music and video file sharing. Operation Payback was orchestrated by Anonymous utilizing distributed denial of service (DDoS) attacks on torrent sites—websites that contain metadata about files and folders spread over a vast number of networks. File-sharing proponents decided to launch DDoS attacks on the most vocal piracy opponents. The initial reaction snowballed into a wave of attacks on major pro-copyright and anti-piracy organizations, law firms, and individuals.

Lizard Squad DDoS attacks and website defacements in 2014

The Lizard Squad is a black hat hacking group, mainly known for their claims of distributed denial-of-service (DDoS) attacks primarily to disrupt interactive gaming related services.

On September 3, 2014, Lizard Squad falsely announced that it had disbanded only to return later on, claiming responsibility for a variety of attacks on prominent websites during the holiday season. Victims included the Sony PlayStation Network, the Xbox Live network, and online gaming participants of League of Legends and Destiny.

Sony Pictures Entertainment in November 2014

The Sony Pictures Entertainment hack was a release of confidential data belonging to Sony Pictures Entertainment on November 24, 2014. The data included personal information about Sony Pictures employees and their families, e-mails between employees, information about executive salaries at the company, copies of previously unreleased Sony films, and other information. The hackers called themselves the *Guardians of Peace* and demanded the cancelation of the planned release of the movie *The Interview*, a comedy about a plot to assassinate North Korean leader Kim Jong-un. United States intelligence officials, evaluating the software, techniques, and network sources used in the hack, allege that the attack was sponsored by North Korea. Naturally, North Korea has denied all responsibility, and some cybersecurity experts have cast doubt on the evidence, alternatively proposing that current or former Sony Pictures employees may have been involved in the hack.

The Sony Pictures case is an excellent example of the problems of attribution. The United States government, which quickly referred to the Sony attack as cyber vandalism, launched an intense investigation and were still unable to point a finger of blame.

Cyber Espionage

Much of what the public, politicians or security vendors attribute to *cyber-terrorism* or *cyber war* is *cyber espionage*, a real and quantifiable type of cyber attack that offers plenty of legitimate examples. An eloquent definition comes from James Clapper, Director of National Intelligence in which he refers to cyber espionage as *intrusions into networks to access sensitive diplomatic, military, or economic information.*

There have been several high-profile cases in which hackers, sanctioned by the Chinese government, infiltrated US companies, including Google and The New York Times, with the intention of stealing corporate secrets from firms that operate in business sectors in which China lags behind. These are examples of corporate or economic espionage, and there are many more players – not just China.

Cyber spies also work in a manner similar to the methods used throughout history. Sun-Tzu infiltrated his military opponents with moles. Undercover espionage was prevalent during the Greek and Roman empires and were employed by ancient governments to further political goals and information gathering. Many examples exist, from propaganda campaigns to malware that has been specifically targeted against an adversary's computing equipment.

For example, the Flame virus is a very sophisticated malware package that records through a PC's microphones, takes screenshots, eavesdrops on Skype conversations, and sniffs network traffic. Iran and other Middle East countries were targeted until the malware was discovered and made public. The United States is suspected as the perpetrator.

After WikiLeaks, the Snowden documents revealed many eavesdropping and espionage programs perpetrated against both US citizens and adversaries abroad by the NSA. The programs, too numerous to name here, are broad and use a wide variety of methods and technologies.

Cyber Warfare

Nineteenth-century Prussian general and military theorist Carl von Clausewitz stated, *War is a mere continuation of policy by other means.* Today, rogue nations and a number of private actors use cyber intrusions as a means of attaining policy goals. These goals often include stealing sensitive corporate data, disrupting information technology systems, and reconnoitering the cyber networks of potential military adversaries. In the same way that ships patrolling coastal waters or infantry prodding along ill-defined borders risked sparking conflict throughout modern history, today's aggressive use of cyber warfare has led to diplomatic clashes, and the threat of escalation.

Cyber warfare, utilizing the Clausewitz theories, is the use of computers by a nation state for an extended, cross-sector interruption of an opponent's activities, especially through the use of deliberate attacks on their information technology or critical infrastructure systems. This definition excludes minor acts of cyber vandalism such as DDoS attacks, and also the collection of information from the adversaries' network systems.

Due to the lack of a broadly accepted definition via an international treaty or established set of guidelines, limiting the definition of cyber warfare is the norm. At the same time it's challenging because definitions can't cover every contingency and are of limited use in gray areas.

International organizations and governments have taken various and often cryptic steps to try to define doctrine for their self-serving approach to cyber war.

A recently published NATO manual on the applicability of international law to cyber warfare does not explicitly define the term, although it does distinguish between *cyber warfare* and *cyber operations*. In it, *cyber weapons* are defined as those that can destroy objects and injure or kill people. Recently a NATO official said a cyber attack on one NATO member could be treated as the equivalent of an armed attack that will be responded to by all NATO allies. But the nature of the NATO response will be decided by allies on a case-by-case basis.

President Obama in 2013 issued a classified Presidential Policy Directive that authorizes military and intelligence agencies to identify likely overseas targets for U.S. cyber attacks. The document permits military commanders to launch cyber attacks to respond to the *threat of an imminent attack* or an emergency situation.

Apparently, the U.S. is following the lead of the Israelis. The Israeli Defense Forces say their military directives handle the event in cyberspace *similarly to other battlefields on the ground, at sea, in the air, and space*. Israel acknowledges that it engages in cyber activity consistently and relentlessly, gathering intelligence and defending its cyberspace. The IDF unabashedly states it is prepared to use cyber space if necessary to execute attacks and intelligence operations—both in defense and part of its military capabilities.

For more than ten years, China's military doctrine has been

relatively explicit on the issue of cyber warfare. China sees the use of cyber intelligence as a methodology whose primary purpose is *to seize and maintain information dominance*. Chinese military tacticians recommend the use of cyber weapons to deceive the enemy or apply psychological pressure on its adversaries.

Russian operations in this area reflect a desire to disrupt information systems of a nation-state while engaging in a disinformation campaign. Russian definitions avoid the term *cyber*. This Russian semantics may indicate a preference for establishing control of internal and external messaging on issues of importance to Moscow. The importance of their messaging became evident in the Russia-Georgia border war of 2007.

CHAPTER TWO
RECENT CYBER SKIRMISHES

A nation's intelligence services use cyber tools to conduct the sort of sensitive tasks that, until recently, were carried out by more traditional means of espionage—spies, commandos, or missiles. Two examples indicate how such actions can disrupt military and economic infrastructure as efficiently as kinetic strikes.

In preparation for the Russia-Georgia border war in 2007, Russian hackers covertly penetrated the internet infrastructure of Georgia to deploy an array of DDOS attacks, logic bombs, and other cyber tools. Once the hot war began, the cyber weapons disabled the Tbilisi government and paralyzed Georgia's financial system. The resulting uncerainty lead to a de facto international banking quarantine as international lenders and other payments processors feared infection from the cyber attack.

The United States and Israel designed the Stuxnet computer worm and remotely introduced it into industrial control systems of Iran that were critical to the country's nuclear program. A long series of unfortunate accidents severely disrupted the Iranian nuclear program. Administration estimates reveal the Iranian nuclear program was set back by a couple of years.

The use of cyber attacks can make espionage appear so widespread and systematic that it creates a climate of insecurity resulting in increased public demands for a robust response. According to a 2013 study, Chinese cyber divisions have conducted espionage operations against nearly 200 American companies since 2006, pirating hundreds of terabytes of data. The Chinese cyber unit, located in Shanghai, apparently have been no direct human collaborators in the targeted companies. The media broadly covered this report coupled with other allegations of rampant Chinese cyber espionage. Enhanced public awareness played a role in the U.S. Department of Justice decision to indict Chinese military intelligence officers for cyber espionage. As a result of the public outcry, calls to engage in offensive cyber operations and take other stiff measures have increased.

Then there are the hacktivists. Hacker groups with ambiguous relationships to nation-states often play a clandestine role in cyber warfare. They provide cover for a government's cyber activities. They are useful cyber proxies in cyber warfare.

The Russians are notorious for using criminal groups and other hackers with no overt links to the Russian Government. Russian cyber operations against Ukraine this year, Georgia in 2008, and Estonia in 2007 appear to have been carried out for the most part by unassociated hackers—although the affected governments and independent security researchers have charged a relationship exists.

China apparently tolerates and encourages *patriotic hackers* who have disrupted the computer networks of U.S., Japanese, and other organizations at times of diplomatic tension.

Finally, there is the ARAMCO cyber attack. Saudi Aramco, officially the Saudi Arabian Oil Company, most popularly known just as Aramco is a Saudi Arabian national petroleum and natural gas company based in Dhahran, Saudi Arabia. In 2012, the hackers, acting under the direction of the Iranian Government, attacked the websites and communications networks of the energy giant ARAMCO. The Saudi Aramco attack by the Iranians were purportedly carried out by independent hacker groups who infiltrated and disrupted political opposition groups' websites.

Like many cyber intrusions, one of the computer technicians on Saudi ARAMCO's information technology team opened a scam email and clicked on a malicious link. The hackers were in.

The actual attack began during the Islamic holy month of Ramadan when most Saudi ARAMCO employees were on holiday. On the morning of Wednesday, Aug. 15, 2012, the few employees noticed their computers were acting weird. Screens started flickering.

Files began to disappear. Some machines just shut down without explanation.

That morning, a group calling itself *Cutting Sword of Justice* claimed responsibility, citing ARAMCO 's support of the Al Saud royal family's authoritarian regime.

"This is a warning to the tyrants of this country and other countries that support such criminal disasters with injustice and oppression," the group said.

In a matter of hours, 35,000 computers were partially wiped or entirely destroyed. Without a way to pay them, gasoline tank trucks seeking refills had to be turned away. ARAMCO's ability to supply ten percent of the world's oil was suddenly at risk.

And one of the most valuable companies on Earth was propelled back into 1970s technology, using typewriters and faxes.

In a frantic rush, Saudi Aramco's computer technicians ripped cables out of computer servers at data centers all over the world. Every office was physically unplugged from the Internet to prevent the virus from spreading further.

Oil production remained steady at 9.5 million barrels per day, according to company records. Drilling and pumping of petroleum were automated, but the rest of the operation was in turmoil. Managing supplies, shipping, contracts with governments and business partners—all of that was forced to happen on paper.

Without the internet at the office, corporate email was gone. Office phones were dead. Employees wrote reports on typewriters. Contracts were passed around with interoffice mail. Lengthy, lucrative deals needing signatures were faxed one page at a time.

The company temporarily stopped selling oil to domestic gas tank trucks. After 17 days, the corporation relented and started giving oil away for free to keep it flowing within Saudi Arabia.

The capabilities and scope of cyber attacks are just now starting to become understood by the public at large – in many cases, like Saudi ARAMCO, quite some time after an attack has taken place. These events have raised awareness within the informational technology sector and the government. A common language and lexicon must be established so that security issues can be shared between the private and public sectors, and with law enforcement, without the contrived anxiety, uncertainty and doubt that is perpetuated by politicians.

CHAPTER THREE
THE FOURTH DIMENSION OF WARFARE

Cyber warfare continues to spread online although the spread of malicious online viruses may just be a precursor to the future of war.

"We operate in five domains: air, land, sea, and cyberspace," says Dan Kuehl, who manages information operations at the National Defense University in Washington, D.C. Kuehl admitted in an interview that a proficient hacker entering keystrokes on a computer is one of the new faces of war—*every bit as powerful as tanks and missiles.* Accordingly, Cyber War is now called the *Fourth Dimension of Warfare.*

A cyber war refers to conducting and preparing to conduct, military operations according to information-related principles. It means disrupting if not destroying the information and communications systems. The term is broadly defined to include even military culture on which an adversary relies in order to *know itself* — who it is, where it is, what it can do when, why it is fighting, which threats to encounter first, etc. It means trying to know all about the enemy while keeping the adversary from knowing much about oneself. It means turning the balance of observations and information in one's favor, especially if the balance of military prowess is not. It means using intelligence so less military capital and labor may have to be expended.

This fourth dimension of warfare involves varied technologies— notably for intelligence collection, processing, and distribution; for tactical communications, positioning, and identification; and for smart weapons systems. This new aspect of warfare has a profound effect on military strategies, tactics, and weapons design. It can be used for defensive or offensive purposes and in all types of conflicts.

As an innovation of conflict, cyber warfare may be the twenty-first century equivalent of what *blitzkrieg* was to the twentieth-century battle fronts. The postmodern battlefield stands to be fundamentally altered by the information technology revolution, at both the strategic and the tactical levels. Even though its full design and implementation require advanced technology, cyber warfare is not reliant on advanced technology per se. A cyber war, whether waged by the United States or other actors, does not necessarily require the presence of advanced technology. The organizational and psychological dimensions may be as important as the technical.

PART TWO

The History and Early Uses of Cyber Warfare

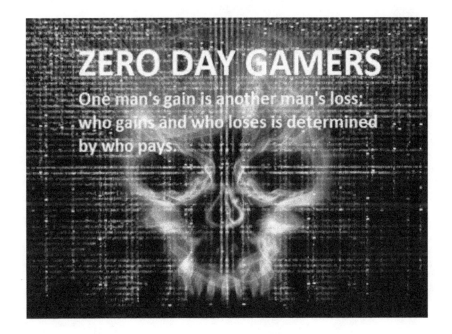

CHAPTER FOUR
HISTORY OF CYBER WARFARE

For as long as the internet has been existence, vandals, spies and criminals have tried to exploit it. Early on, computer hacker Kevin Mitnick became a top target for the FBI for breaking into academic and corporate computer systems and causing millions of dollars in damage. After years of avoiding capture, he spent five years behind bars in the 1990s and was ordered to stay away from computers for three additional years while on probation. The *Melissa* and *I Love You* viruses of the late nineties drew widespread attention to expanding cyber threats and jump-started the sale of internet security software that is now a multibillion-dollar industry.

Cyber attacks have grown more frequent and destructive in recent years. One form of hacking — the denial-of-service (DoS) attack — has become a tool of war. The attacks are designed to paralyze websites, financial networks, and other computer systems by flooding them with data from outside computers. A fifteen-year-old Canadian with the moniker *mafiaboy* launched the first documented DoS attack in 2000 against eBay and Amazon.com, shutting some down and wreaking havoc that cost an estimated $1.7 billion. In 2007, entities believed to have been associated with the Russian government or its allies launched a DoS attack against the nation of Estonia. The cyber attack was undertaken as a result of a dispute sparked by the removal of a World War II–era Soviet soldier from a public park. The attacks crippled the Estonia's digital infrastructure, paralyzed government and media sites, and shut down the former Soviet Republic's largest bank. As discussed previously, a massive cyber attack against Georgia is believed to have taken place before Russia's invasion of the country in 2008, crippling the banking system and disrupting cell-phone service.

Government and private Web networks in the U.S. have emerged as frequent targets for those flouting the law. The Pentagon reported some four hundred million attempts to break into its computer systems in 2014, up from just six million in 2006. The intrusions include a successful attempt to hack into the $300 billion Joint Strike Fighter project and copy data about the aircraft's design and electronics systems. The espionage is believed to have originated in China.

Experts say computer criminals in China and Russia have also infiltrated America's electrical grid, covertly installing software with the potential to damage it at any time (naturally, both countries have denied such actions). The Pentagon has plans to quadruple the ranks of its cybersecurity experts, explaining that the country is under cyber attack all the time, every day.

Cyber spies also targeted regular citizens. News Headlines regularly tell of hackers ransacking computer networks for Social Security numbers, banking information and other data that could be used for potential identity theft. In a recent example, officials at the University of California, Berkeley, reported hackers stole the Social Security numbers of nearly all of its students, alumni and others during a six-month breach of the school's computer system. Other computer vandals have caused physical harm. A forum run by the Epilepsy Foundation had to be shut down after online intruders, in perhaps the nastiest prank yet, led visitors to sites featuring bright, flashing images known to potentially trigger seizures. Over recent years, cyber threats have become very diverse, and attacks have become more frequent and successful, highlighting the failure of government agencies and private institutions to protect themselves.

But it was July of 2010 that STUXNET marked the moment when Cyber Warfare became a reality—an attack originating in cyberspace targeting a part of a nation's critical national infrastructure. The complexity of STUXNET suggests that the governments of Israel and the U.S. were heavily involved in its development. As a result, there are massive implications for how future wars will be fought, with conflict set to be characterized by a dual campaign in cyberspace and reality.

CHAPTER FIVE
SIGNIFICANT EVENTS IN THE HISTORY
OF CYBER WARFARE

The Trans-Siberian Soviet Pipeline Sabotage, 1982

Thomas C. Reed, a former Air Force secretary who served on President Ronald Reagan's National Security Council, wrote about the event in *At the Abyss: An Insider's History of the Cold War*. He summarized the operation as one example of *cold-eyed economic warfare*. In 1982, the Soviets actively pirated American software programs and technology to be used in the service of the former Soviet Union's gas supply. American intelligence became aware of this activity and in order to sabotage the Soviet efforts and disrupt their economy, the pipeline software utilized to run the pumps, turbines, and valves was programmed to malfunction, after a decent interval, to reset pump speeds and valve settings to produce pressures far beyond those acceptable to pipeline joints and welds. The result was the largest non-nuclear explosion and fire ever seen from space.

While there were no physical casualties from the pipeline explosion, there was significant damage to the Soviet economy. Its ultimate bankruptcy, not a bloody battle or nuclear exchange, helped bring the Cold War to an end. In time, the Soviets came to understand that they had been stealing bogus technology, but now what were they to do? By implication, the Soviets believed every aspect of their infrastructure might be infected. They had no way of knowing which software was sound, which was infected. All was suspect, which was the intended endgame for the operation.

The faulty software was provided to the Russians after an agent recruited by the French and dubbed Farewell provided a shopping list of Soviet priorities, which focused on stealing Western technology. The software, which was *allowed* to be pirated, contained malfunctions resulting in the shutdown of many aspects of the Soviet critical infrastructure.

Kosovo War, May 7, 1999

The Kosovo conflict started in 1998 between Yugoslavian police and military forces and Albanian separatists in Kosovo. As the conflict spread, NATO launched an air strike campaign against Yugoslavia. The air strikes lasted for 78 days, after which Yugoslavia agreed to withdraw its forces out of Kosovo.

This was one of the first military conflicts with an extensive use of cyber activity. Many cyber attacks happened during the 78-day war. However, even though the military conflict ended after the Kumanovo peace treaty, the conflict remained in cyberspace as the cyber war continued between Serbian and Albanian hackers trying to disrupt internet websites and infrastructure of the other side for years. Eventually, NATO became the target as NATO suffered attacks on its computer systems from Serbia.

Estonia, May 2007

The Estonian virtual invasion consisted of distributed denial-of-service attacks. With DDoS attacks, hackers use other people's computers, sometimes halfway across the globe, to wreak virtual havoc. To launch DDoS attacks, hackers first access other people's computers through zombie applications, malicious software that overrides security measures or creates an entry point. Once hackers gain control over the so-called zombie computers, they can network them together to form cyber-armies or botnets. The Estonian attack relied on vast botnets to send the coordinated crash-inducing data to the Web servers. It was complex and efficient.

Hackers believed to be linked to the Russian government brought down the Web sites of Estonia's parliament, banks, ministries, newspapers, and broadcasters. Cyber warriors blocked the websites of the Estonian government and clogged the country's Internet network. The attacks disrupted the use of Estonia's websites for 22 days.

Russo – Georgia War, August 2008

Cyber attackers hijacked government and commercial web sites in Georgia during a military conflict with Russia. Russian forces invaded Georgia, preceded by cyber attacks on Georgian government and business websites and network infrastructure, disabling the country's Web-based communication with the outside world.

Cyber attacks continue to grow in number and sophistication each year. In 2006, Russian Mafia group Russian Business Network (RBN) began using malware for identity theft. By 2007, RBN completely monopolized online identity theft. By September 2007, their Storm Worm was estimated to be running on roughly one million computers, sending millions of infected emails each day.

In 2008, cyber attacks moved from personal computers to government institutions. On August 27, 2008, NASA confirmed a worm was found on laptops in the International Space Station; three months later Pentagon computers were hacked, allegedly by Russian hackers.

Financial institutions were next. The State Bank of India—India's largest bank, was attacked by hackers located in Pakistan on December 25, 2008. While no data was lost, the attack forced the bank to temporarily shut down their website and resolve the issue.

Today, the use of cyber intrusion has grown to become the most potent weapon in many nations' arsenals. As such, there are now three main methods of cyber warfare that have evolved—*sabotage, electronic espionage,* and *attacks on electrical power grids.* The third is perhaps most alarming and the U. S. is especially vulnerable. In 2012, the North American Electric Reliability Corporation (NERC) warned the U.S. electrical grid is susceptible to cyber attacks, which could lead to massive power outages, delayed military response, and economic disruption. Destruction of critical infrastructure will be the goals of hackers shortly.

PART THREE

PRESENT DAY USE OF CYBER WARFARE

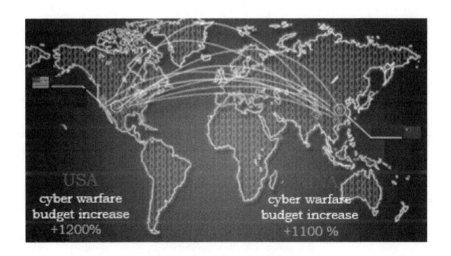

CHAPTER SIX
MAJOR PLAYERS

First, a Note on the Hacker Culture

In general, hackers in the West are often anti-government and activists. They're not usually patriotic, they're not usually nationalistic, and often the majority of their cyber activities are considered criminal at worst, and cyber vandalism at best. In the East, hackers are pro-government, and their activities are ignored, if not condoned, by their governments. Countries like Iran, North Korea, and China are havens for cyber activity—which are deemed patriotic and nationalistic.

Who are the main actors?

CHINA

Governments have always kept secrets. Governments have always spied. But the dramatic focus on technological advances in cyber espionage and hacking is shifting the battle lines of the 21st century.

Cyber attacks have now joined the traditional weapons of government. Nation-states are exploiting gaps in foreign networks, collecting zero-day vulnerabilities and installing network surveillance as just some of their military and intelligence tactics.

This upsurge in cyber warfare activity is being engaged in openly between the United States and China. In 2015, a secret National Security Agency document uncovered revealed more than six hundred successful attacks by Chinese sources on American private and public networks over a five-year period.

As this cyber war heats up, analysts are now concerned a

diplomatic Armageddon could fast be approaching as the two influential countries show no signs of backing down. It is a relationship characterized by mistrust between China and the U.S. The two countries have always maintained a strained relationship when the topic is discussed.

The interests of the two nations are often fundamentally opposed when it comes to issues of cyber activity and its governance. The U.S. plan calls for transparency and freedom of information while China relies upon state control over information in cyberspace. So far, China and the U.S. have restricted their cyber activities to military and economic espionage, rather than other forms of cyber attacks that might give rise to an act of war.

Recently, however, the cyber relationship between the U.S. and China has worsened with authorities engaged in petty responses to continued allegations of cyber espionage. In May of 2014, Attorney General Eric Holder filed hacking charges against five Chinese nationals for infiltrating US commercial targets by cyber activities. In response, the Beijing government suspended a joint working group on cyber security and began a retaliatory campaign against U.S. technology companies operating in China.

China has always denied any such activities, but that changed this year after the publication of their updated *Science of Military Strategy*, an extraordinary military treatise published by the top research institute of the People's Liberation Army. The treatise acknowledged China's cyber capabilities for the first time. The document contains the military strategy and admits the government is highly motivated in the embracing of cyber espionage and network security.

It reveals that preemptive defenses, precision strike missiles, and cyber warfare, are an integral part of the Chinese military apparatus.

Unsurprisingly, an analysis of the document found the United States is the primary target of the PLA's cyber warfare efforts.

Clearly, the US is China's main strategic adversary. Beijing believes Washington is actively trying to limit China's economic and military development. The Chinese maintain the United States is restricting its freedom of action internationally by using a broad combination of financial, diplomatic and military pressure.

An analysis of the Chinese policy outlined in the Science of Military Strategy reveals a three-pronged approach to cyber warfare.

First, China splits its cyber operations into three sections:

- Specialized military network warfare forces.

- The PLA's authorized forces such as the Ministry of State Security and the Ministry of Public Security.

- The non-governmental force of hackers who don't officially work for the government but can be called into action when needed—the patriots.

It is this third category that is of concern to many rival nation-states given some of the victims targeted by this *unaffiliated* group of *patriots*.

"There is a spectrum of state sponsorship," says Jen Weedon with FireEye, a world leader in cyber security. "There is certainly activity that we see that appears to be very state directed and then there's activity we see and research we have done on particular actors that indicate there are also contractors doing this activity and everything in between."

"We have seen some elements of cyber tools, logistics and supply chains. For example, we have seen individual pieces of malware or backdoors that appear to be shared by a lot of different groups and may be getting it from a single source. There's clearly quite an extensive infrastructure behind this behavior," says Sean Sullivan, security advisor at F-Secure. He further argues that while these hacking groups often seem to work in the interests of China, there's no guarantee this will last indefinitely.

The vast majority of Chinese hacking is done by individuals politically sympathetic to China. Not all of it is directed by the state. Why don't Chinese hackers target China? Thus far, the economy is performing too well. Double-digit growth keeps their citizens happy and *patriotic*. Losing control of this talent is something that the

Chinese government must be very concerned about.

The blurry line of the law

The Science of Military Strategy treatise elevates the nature of the threat to the United States, the West, and its businesses. It also illustrates the threat posed by the fact Chinese hackers steal intelligence and intellectual property.

Sullivan notes that this is a fundamental difference in how China acts in the cyber arena, when compared to the U.S.

"When the US spies, it does so to level the playing field. In a well-known example, the U.S. spied on Airbus to prevent bribes in the Middle East. But, according to the US, no intellectual property was transferred from Airbus to Boeing. China doesn't see the distinction," he said.

This is an example of how the usual rules and treaties that apply to armed conflicts and intelligence have not been extended to cyber warfare.

"There aren't any international agreements governing *peacetime* intelligence gathering," Sullivan said. "Cyber technologies have changed the nature of intelligence gathering. And perhaps it's time to write some new treaties of what's acceptable and what's not."

Is there a red line that can be crossed?

The need for such treaties in the cyber realm was underlined in 2015 after the breach at the US Office of Personnel Management (OPM), perhaps the most high-profile case of cyber-espionage in recent times.

The OPM revealed that over 21.5 million federal records had been stolen, including Social Security numbers, education history, employment history, and financial background of federal employees. Later in 2015, the OPM admitted nearly six million fingerprints were also obtained via a different cyber intrusion. FBI Director James Comey said in a US Senate appearance that even his information was likely to have been compromised, showing the full scope of the breach.

Unsurprisingly China is believed to have carried out the hack, although it was not publically accused of doing so.

A senior research fellow for military influence at the Royal United Services Institute explained the sheer scale of the attack led to a serious debate in the West about how to deal with China and the growing cyber crisis.

Perhaps it is time to draw a *red line* about what is acceptable. Although many argue the U.S. must be cautious about the extent to which this might constrain its activities. There is a sense that the scale and frequency of attacks apparently emanating from China has reached a level where, even if the purpose is *traditional espionage*, it is no longer acceptable and requires a response in kind.

China has denied any involvement in the OPM hack and was able to make its accusations directed at the U.S. alleging state-sponsored spying. Chinese foreign ministry spokesman Lu Kang said, "maybe it is better to clarify one's matters before rushing to make unfounded accusations against others, so as to make oneself sound more convincing."

Perhaps Lu was referring to the disclosures made by former NSA contractor Edward Snowden in 2013. The whistle-blower released a trove of classified documents detailing mass surveillance programs run by the US and UK governments.

The Snowden disclosure changed how the U.S. was perceived around the world and made it hard for the politicians in Washington to act with moral superiority. Much of the American moral high ground was lost through Snowden when the material demonstrated the extent to which the NSA was collecting enormous amounts of data.

As of this writing, President Obama and Chinese President Xi Jinping are meeting to amid growing tensions over Chinese cyber attacks. The President is attemptting to establish a red line—the nation's infrastructure.

Has the President shown his hand as to the biggest threat this country faces?

RUSSIA

Russia is well known for its military mentality. Remember the cold war? It has taken nearly a decade for the world to realize the true threat of cyber war. Today, the world is dependent on computers and networks much more than we were eight years ago when we experienced the NATO-Serbia cyber war. Russia opened the eyes of the world to the looming threat of cyber warfare after the Estonia incident. Now Russia's state-sponsored cyber forces opened up a new front in a cyber war.

Reports indicate Russian *Cyber Forces* unleashed a large-scale cyber attack on Radio Free Europe. Also, there is some evidence of the use of BotNets in politically motivated distributed denial-of-service (DDoS) attacks. This raises questions about Russia's real cyber warfare ambitions Russia's cyber warfare doctrine is designed to be a force multiplier along with more traditional military actions including potential weapons of mass destruction attacks. A force multiplier is a military term that describes a weapon or tactic that, when added to and employed along with other combat forces, significantly increases the combat potential of that force.

Like all offensive cyber strategies, it includes the capability to disruption the information infrastructure of their enemies. This doctrine includes plans that would disrupt financial markets, military, and civilian communications capabilities as well as other parts of the enemy's critical infrastructure prior to the initiation of traditional military operations. They also are designed to weaken the economy of their adversary further decreasing their adversary's ability to respond to the combined threat. Offensive cyber weapons receive considerable attention in the Russian cyber warfare doctrine. This coupled with advanced research and development puts them on the leader board behind China as a cyber threat.

Cyber attacks and cyber weapons are now recognized as strategic arms and in effect are useful offensive weapons. As the Russians have proven in Georgia, Estonia and Ukraine, cyber attacks can harm or even paralyze a country and, therefore, have equivalent implications as that of physical military strikes. Not all cyber attacks leave behind forensic evidence that can be used to assess the capabilities of the attacker. With all the attacks attributed to Russia, there has to be significant intelligence out there about techniques, cyber weapons, and strategies that have been used in these cyber assaults.

Cyber warfare capabilities have outpaced our legal and political systems. Russian President Vladimir Putin has blasted the U.S. for its militaristic approach to foreign policy, saying its actions were *nourishing an arms race.* Consider this evidence of Russia's dedication to cyber capabilities. In 1998, Russia's defense budget was less than $3 billion. Since that time, the Russian defense budget has been soaring, funded by substantial increases in their cyber warfare program, the budget jumped twenty-three percent in 2007 to $32.4 billion.

An interesting point to keep in mind is that Moscow does arms business with over seventy countries, including China, Iran, and Syria. Reports indicate Russian intelligence services have a history of employing hackers from these nations to be used against the United States. For example, in 1985, the KGB hired Markus Hess, an East German hacker, to attack U.S. defense agencies in the infamous case of the Cuckoo's Egg.

The following is an estimate of Russia's cyber capabilities.

Russia's Cyber Army:
Military Budget: $40 Billion USD
Global Rating in Cyber Capabilities: Tied at Number 4
Cyber Warfare Budget: $127 Million USD
Offensive Cyber Capabilities: Significant
Cyber Weapons Arsenal in Order of Threat:
•Large, advanced BotNet for DDoS and espionage
•Electromagnetic pulse weapons (non-nuclear)
•Compromised counterfeit computer software
•Advanced dynamic exploitation capabilities
•Wireless data communications jammers
•Cyber Logic Bombs Computer viruses and worms

•Cyber data collection exploits Computer and networks reconnaissance tools

•Embedded Trojan time bombs (suspected)

Cyber Force size: 7,300 +

The government in Moscow has established close ties with the Russian Business Network, which is thought to own and operate the second largest BotNet in the world. Intelligence suggests there are organized groups of hackers tied to the Russian Federal Security Bureau. The FSB is the internal counterintelligence agency of the Russian Federation and successor to the Soviet KGB. Russia is often overlooked as a significant player in the global software industry although it produces two hundred thousand scientific and technology graduates each year. The number of graduates are as many as India, which has five times the population.

A study by the World Bank states that more than one million people are involved in software research and development. Russia has the potential to become one of the largest internet technology markets in Eurasia. The Russian hacker attack on Estonia in 2007 rang the alarm bell. Nations around the world can no longer ignore the advanced threat that Russia's cyber warfare capabilities have today and the ones they aspire to have shortly.

From this information, one can only conclude that Russia has advanced capabilities and the intent and technological capabilities necessary to carry out cyber warfare anywhere in the world at any time.

IRAN

Iran has been steadily developing its cyber warfare capabilities for a number of years and now poses a significant threat to government agencies and critical infrastructure companies around the world, according to a report entitled *Operation Cleaver* released by U.S. cyber security firm Cylance. The title alludes to the custom software used in Iranian hacking operations, which frequently uses the word *cleaver* in its coding.

Operation Cleaver has targeted the military, oil and gas, energy and utilities, transportation, airlines, airports, hospitals and aerospace industries of over fifty entities in sixteen countries. If the operation is left to continue unabated, it is only a matter of time before the Iranians impact the world's physical safety, Cylance said in its eighty-seven page report.

Iran has officially denied involvement in the hacking campaigns. "This is a baseless and unfounded allegation fabricated to tarnish the Iranian government image, particularly aimed at hampering current nuclear talks," said Hamid Babaei, spokesman for Iran's mission to the United Nations, in an interview with Reuters.

In light of how ambitious Iran's hacking campaigns have become, the report makes a bold claim: Iran is the new China. While Iran's cyber capabilities aren't anywhere near those of Russia, China, or the United States, their program is advancing with the help of the Chinese and Russia.

Iran's hacking campaigns began in earnest in 2011, in retaliation for the cyber attacks that were launched against the country's nuclear program from 2009-2012 by the U.S. and Israel.

The Iranians have learned cyber warfare doesn't require a significant number of troops or a superior set of bombs. In the event of a conflict, Iran will be able to use its cyber technology to shut down critical infrastructure around the world. Following the Russian template, Iran is enhancing its cyber warfare capabilities more for military readiness.

Experts say during Operation Pillar of Defense, Israeli websites faced a larger, more coordinated, and more skilled series of cyber attacks than during similar conflicts. At the same time Hamas, with the assistance of its state sponsor Iran, was trading fire with the Israel Defense Forces, hackers from all over the world launched a string of coordinated attacks on electronic targets in Israel.

According to Gadi Aviran, CEO of the Netanya-based open-source intelligence analysis firm SenseCy/Terrogence, hackers have used the last two Israeli military operations in Gaza as an opportunity to strike at the country. But this time, their efforts revealed a greater level of capability and expertise.

"It was much more profound than previous operations," said Aviran. "The cyber attack was well-organized, had a lot of traction, and it used some more advanced techniques than we saw before. It was a logical step in their cyber-evolution."

This meant a greater frequency of typically unsuccessful or short-lived acts of web vandalism, like the replacement of a web page with a picture of Adolf Hitler or Hezbollah leader Hassan Nasrallah, or attempted data bombs or denial of service attacks. But hackers did manage to overwhelm and slow down an important Israeli internet service provider — a nearly unprecedented accomplishment. In total, almost three thousand Israeli websites were defaced during the attacks, while several databases were leaked online.

The vast majority of attacks didn't originate in Gaza or the West Bank. Many came from hundreds or even thousands of miles from Israel's borders, through surrogates like Morocco and Indonesia.

Iran seems especially determined to prove its cyber capabilities against Israel. With Iran building up its cyber-offensive capabilities during the past decade significantly, Israel now considers Russia, China, and Iran to be the sources of the most aggressive and worrying attacks against its online and electronic infrastructure.

Most Russian-based attacks are criminal in nature — attempts to steal credit card numbers or bank account information. China has a broad-based hacking strategy that involves efforts against ostensibly friendly or at least non-hostile countries, as when Chinese-based hackers attempted to steal information about Israel's Iron Dome missile interceptor system in 2011 and 2012.

Iranian-based hacking is different in nature. Unlike Russia or China, the Iranian government is politically and ideologically opposed not just to Israeli policy, but to the country's very existence. Hacking originating in Iran is aimed at directly undermining Israel in a way that Russian or Chinese hacking typically isn't.

Iran made cyber capabilities a top defense priority after the Stuxnet computer bug, a joint project of Israel and the U.S. that infiltrated and sabotaged Iran's nuclear program. The Iranian government realized that its enemies had brought the fight to a new battlefield and established a dedicated cyber command in 2011 as a result.

There is a precedent for Iran using online Palestinian front groups as a front for anti-Israel activities. In 2013, a group called Qods Freedom, which claimed to be Palestinian, was found responsible for the extensive denial of service attacks on Israeli sites in July and August of that year. But their online vandalism included Arabic mistakes that no native speaker would make, using a tile set that SenseCy determined could only have been produced by a Persian-language keyboard. Qods Freedom also used the same defacement signature as two Iranian groups.

According to the reports, the Hamas-linked Izz al-Din Al Qassam Cyber Fighters were also a product of the military strategy in Tehran.

Iranian hacking is a multi-faceted enterprise. It encompasses hidden proxies like Qods Freedom — but also government-backed, semi-independent groups, like the very proficient Ashiyane Digital Security Team, and internet based subsidiaries of Iranian-supported foreign militant groups, like Cyber Hezbollah.

Iranian-based hackers' capability seems to be catching up to their ambitions. In February of 2014, the Wall Street Journal reported that Iran-based hackers had so deeply infiltrated Navy and Marine Corps unclassified web systems that it would take four months to dislodge them fully.

In 2015, as Iran negotiates a nuclear agreement with the U.S. and its partners, it hasn't scaled back its asymmetrical ambitions — whether on Iraq's sectarian battlefields or on Israeli and American web servers.

NORTH KOREA

Two entities undertake North Korean cyber operations—the Korean People's Army General Staff Department (GSD) and the Reconnaissance General Bureau (RGB). According to South Korean government analysis, the DPRK employs six thousand *cyber warriors* in North Korea.

In 2009, the RGB was formed as a consolidation of various intelligence and special ops units that previously existed throughout the North Korean government. This included portions of the North Korean military apparatus tasked with political warfare, foreign intelligence, propaganda, subversion, kidnapping, special operations, and assassinations. The RGB answers directly to the National Defense Commission and Kim Jong-un in his role as supreme commander of the Korean People's Army.

The RGB is now responsible for extensive operational cyber missions that assist the government in achieving the objectives of its political provocations. The cyber units most frequently linked to RGB are *Unit 121* and *Lab 110*. The English translation—*Unit* or *Lab*—does not accurately reflect their importance within the North Korean military bureaucracy. There are four bureaus comprising the RGB—1st Operations Bureau, 2nd Reconnaissance Bureau, 3rd Foreign Intelligence Bureau, and 6th Technical Bureau. *Unit 121* and *Lab 110* would be subordinate to or synonymous with the 6th Technical Bureau. It is also likely that the 3rd Foreign Intelligence Bureau has a cyber espionage component as well.

Unit 121 has been typically linked to the *DarkSeoul* attack. In March of 2013, three South Korean broadcast networks, and a major bank suffered cyber attacks via malware known as *DarkSeoul*. The malware infected the computer systems so extensively, most had to be replaced and large volumes of data were lost. Because the attacks were routed through proxies located in China, attribution to the North Koreans was not possible.

Lab 110 has been accused of using a bogus information technology company in Shenyang to sell malicious software to South Korean customers. The exact operational relationship between Unit 121 and Lab 110 is not known. There is a possibility that offensive cyber operations could be easily combined with human intelligence or covert operations capability for military purposes.

In North Korea, the General Staff Department (GSD) of the

Korean People's Army (KPA) is broadly comparable to the U.S. Joint Chiefs of Staff and oversees the operational aspects of the entire KPA. As such, it has authority over numerous operational cyber units, including units tasked with political subversion, cyber warfare, and operations such as network defense. North Korea is in the process of assembling these units into an overarching cyber command and control structure. Currently, the GSD's Operations Bureau has been attributed with conducting cyber operations, but intelligence information about the scope of these activities, as well as the various units conducting them, has been spotty.

Kim Jong-un directly oversees the GSD's position in government. Analysts surmise that the bulk of North Korea's offensive cyber operations is housed in RGB, a black operations organization. Because its GSD missions stem from electronic warfare, this portends strong implications for what the North Koreans tend to target, what type of attack they rely on, and what mission they hope to achieve via cyber warfare.

Pursuant to the claims of people who have escaped into South Korea, their primary target is Western critical infrastructure. The cyber army on Unit 121 is trained and operates for this primary purpose.

It is widely known that North Korea has the highest percentage of military personnel in relation to population—roughly forty enlisted soldiers per thousand people.

In 2013, a defector declared that North Korea was increasing its cyber warfare unit to staff eight thousand people, and it was undertaking a massive training program for its young prodigies to become proficient in cyber warfare.

Last year, new revelations on the cyber capabilities of North Korea confirmed that the government of Pyongyang doubled the number of the units of its cyber army. According to reports, the number of cyber warriors of the North Korea has also established overseas bases for hacking attacks.

North Korea wants to demonstrate its cyber capabilities to the rest of the world. According to reports, a Stuxnet-style attack designed to destroy a city has been prepared by North Korea and is a feasible threat to the smart grids of the United States.

According to intelligence agencies, North Korean hackers are responsible for numerous cyber attacks worldwide, including the clamorous Sony hack and a targeted offensive on South Korea Hydro and Nuclear Power Plant. Although the nuclear plant was not compromised by the attack, if the computer system controlling the nuclear reactor were compromised, the consequences could be unimaginably severe and cause extensive casualties.

Clearly, if North Korea continues to escalate its cyber attacks on a critical infrastructure, it's only a matter of time before significant loss of life occurs.

SYRIAN ELECTRONIC ARMY

The Syrian Electronic Army (commonly known as the "SEA") is a group of computer hackers which first surfaced online in 2011 to support the government of Syrian President Bashar al-Assad. Using spamming, website defacement, malware, phishing, and denial of service attacks, it has targeted political opposition groups, Western news organizations, human rights groups and websites that are seemingly neutral to the Syrian conflict. It has also hacked government websites in the Middle East and Europe, as well as US defense contractors. According to U.S. intelligence agencies, the SEA has become the first Arab country to have a state-sponsored *internet army* hosted on its national networks to openly launch cyber attacks on its enemies.

The SEA has focused its cyber activities in four key areas:

Use of website defacement and electronic surveillance against its adversaries—namely the Syrian rebels. The SEA has carried out surveillance to discover the identities and location of Syrian rebels, using malware, phishing, and denial of service attacks.

Defacement attacks against Western media websites based on the belief these sites spread news adverse to the interests of the

Syrian government. Targeted companies include news websites such as BBC News, the Associated Press, National Public Radio, CBC News, Al Jazeera, Financial Times, The Daily Telegraph, The Washington Post, Syrian satellite broadcaster Orient TV, and Dubai-based al-Arabia TV, as well as rights organizations such as Human Rights Watch.

Spamming popular Facebook pages with pro-regime comments. The Facebook pages of President Barack Obama and former French President Nicolas Sarkozy have been targeted by SEA spam campaigns.

Global cyber espionage is another function of the SEA. Technology and media companies, allied military procurement officers, US defense contractors, and foreign attaches and embassies have all fallen victim to the SEA's cyber vandalism.

The SEA's tone and style vary from the serious and openly political to ironic statements intended as critical or pointed humor. For example, the SEA tweeted from the Twitter account of 60 Minutes the following: *Exclusive: Terror is striking the #USA and #Obama is Shamelessly in Bed with Al-Qaeda.* In July 2012, the SEA posted from Al Jazeera's Twitter account: *Do you think Saudi and Qatar should keep funding armed gangs in Syria in order to topple the government?* In another attack, members of SEA used the BBC Weather Channel Twitter account to post the headline: *Saudi weather station down due to head on-collision with a camel.*

U.S. analysts rank Syria well behind the top four of China, Russia, Iran and North Korea in its cyber capabilities. They are considered at the vandalism level. But the recent interjection of Russia into the Syrian crisis in 2015 leads many to believe that the government of Bashar al-Assad will receive a boost in its cyber programs courtesy of advanced Russian technologies.

ISIS

Islamic terrorists have threatened an all-out cyber war against the United States, and experts say the warnings should be taken seriously.

Hackers claiming affiliation with the ISIS released a video in the spring of 2015 vowing an *electronic war* against the West and claiming access to *American leadership* online.

"Praise to Allah, today we extend on the land and on the Internet," a faceless, hooded figure said in Arabic. "We send this message to America and Europe: We are the hackers of the Islamic State, and the electronic war has not yet begun."

As hackers around the world become more sophisticated, terrorist groups are likely to emulate their activities. It's only really a matter of time until terrorist organizations begin using cyber techniques in a more expanded way. As an organization like ISIS acquires more resources financially, they will be able to hire the talent they need or outsource to criminal organizations.

Military officials agree. Director of the National Security Agency, Admiral Michael Rogers, called the pending shift a great concern and something that the U.S. military and intelligence communities pay lots of attention to.

"At what point do they decide they need to move from viewing the Internet as a source of recruitment ... [to] viewing it as a potential weapon system?" Rogers asked.

While ISIS has been widely recognized for its social media recruiting capabilities, the growing computer science talent of its recruits has mostly gone unnoticed. Some of the individuals that have recently joined the movement of ISIS are students of computer science in British schools and European universities. As a result, the cyber capabilities of ISIS are advancing dramatically. Even the man reportedly responsible for a number of the brutal ISIS beheadings, dubbed *Jihadi John* by his captives, has a computer science degree.

Part of the danger of the ISIS threat is the group's ability to marshal attacks from its sympathizers, generating an unconnected network that is hard to track.

ISIS effectively uses the video threats as a *call to arms* meant to incite individuals to act on their own. It has added a new dimension to the terrorist threat that the U.S. counterterrorism approach is not intended or designed to pick up on. For example, ISIS supporters have focused on distributed denial-of-service attacks, spear phishing campaigns and the hijacking of legitimate websites to push malware, creating what are known as *watering holes*. In a watering hole attack, the attacker analyzes their victims browsing habits and affects those sites with malware. As the targeted victim frequents the site, their networks become infected.

For example, if you go to an ISIS friendly website and download their videos, you better recognize most of those websites are watering holes. ISIS installed malware will attack your network while you're watching their video. Experts think radical hackers are likely to expand this tactic to mainstream websites and powerful companies' websites as a way to gather information on targets.

ISIS is beginning to conduct more and more counterintelligence using this method. Their use of the internet has been described as unprecedented for a terrorist group, and lawmakers are growing increasingly concerned about U.S. attempts to counter its rhetoric online.

Most of ISIS's current online power lies in its messaging; experts say, and not in its ability to hack real computer networks. But a handful of high-profile intrusions points toward its aspirations as a hacking group. The so-called *Cyber Caliphate* took over the Twitter and YouTube accounts for the U.S. Central Command in January 2015, and the Twitter account for Newsweek magazine in a month after that.

In March of 2015, the *Islamic State Hacking Division* of ISIS posted the personal details of hundreds of U.S. military personnel supposedly involved in attacks on ISIS in Iraq and Syria.

One such message read: *With the huge amount of data we have from various servers and databases, we have decided to leak 100 addresses so that our brothers in America can deal with you...Kill them in their own lands, behead them in their own homes, stab them to death as they walk their streets thinking that they are safe.*

Within two months of the posting, a terrorist inspired gunman attacked military recruitment facilities in Chattanooga, Tennessee killing several service members.

In April of 2015, a French TV station was knocked offline in perhaps the best example of terrorists' abilities. "It seemed to be on a broader scale than we had seen previously," said a U. S. State Department official. "There were a number of facets to that attack, and they also took the station offline for quite a while. That seemed to me to be of a different magnitude." The group managed to orchestrate a complete three-hour blackout of the French channel TV5Monde. They hacked into all 11 channels run by the company, along with its website and social media outlets. While the attack took place, the hackers placed documents on TV5Monde's Facebook page, which they claimed were classified dossiers of relatives of French soldiers involved in fighting ISIS. The Islamic State Hacking Division again claimed responsibility.

As the cyber capabilities and successes of ISIS escalate, many analysts believe the next step is inevitable. There is evidence of an increase in ISIS activity on the *cyber arms bazaar*, the massive underground black hat web market based in Eastern Europe that traffics in almost every form of cyber sabotage imaginable. It is only a matter of time before we hear about significant attacks that were pulled off by sympathizers of ISIS.

The nature of ISIS's online presence is intended to do three things. Firs, and most importantly for the longevity of its existence, it's designed as a mechanism to attract and recruit members to its ranks. Second, it's a means through which ISIS aims to strike fear into the hearts of all that come across its frequently gruesome propaganda. Both objectives are well documented. A third important dimension to the ISIS presence online is emerging. ISIS utilizes cyberspace for offensive purposes—to use the cyber domain to disrupt services, damage reputations and reveal sensitive data.

The cyber attacks of 2015 orchestrated by ISIS illustrate the group's increased degree of sophistication. There had clearly been an amount of pre-attack planning, including a level of social engineering that had gone on to completely shut down the station's computer systems. ISIS, and those claiming to support the group are now looking to take their cyber offensive to the next level.

Should we be worried about the self-styled Cyber Caliphate and the potential for ISIS to launch highly sophisticated attacks against sensitive networks, similar to the STUXNET virus that was unleashed on Iran? At present, despite a clear elevation in capability, the answer may be *soon, but not yet*. Attacks of the magnitude of STUXNET require a level of financing, highly-skilled personnel and human intelligence gathering that an organization such as ISIS simply doesn't possess. The more likely scenario is that websites will continue to be defaced and social media accounts hacked, to influence sympathetic supporters.

But that's no reason to be complacent about ISIS' capabilities and its intent. The cyber domain provides a group like ISIS with a low-cost means of harassing their adversaries and promoting their cause. They've demonstrated an ability to utilize modern technology and unleash effective propaganda, and they've proven attractive to *tech-savvy* youngsters. With their 2015 successes, confidence will have increased, and the next attack will be planned with greater ambition. There's no reason that ISIS won't work to mature what has so far been a successful strategy and capability. In many ways this reflects what we see in the broader cyber threat environment: the cyber domain is becoming an essential part of offensive operations for any group, be it a government, criminal organization or terrorist group. Over the last five months, ISIS has shown us that they are pushing to close the knowledge and capability gap when it comes to offensive cyber operations.

We'd be wise to keep a close watch.

PART FOUR

UNITED STATES POLICY, PROBLEM OF ATTRIBUTION, DEFENSE DEPARTMENT PREPARATIONS

CHAPTER SEVEN
UNITED STATES POLICY STANCE;
THE FIVE PILLARS

The United States, like many of its Western counterparts, has lost control of the technology upon which the power, as well as the threats to national security within our respective governments, rest. The cyber arena, and the technology upon which it is based, includes the science of cyber engineering. The safety aspects of this science have been evolved into the weapons that will be used as the primary offensive assets in the upcoming new age of cyber warfare.

The next major war will not be fought with tanks, vessels, and cruise missiles. The world will experience a cyber war with the potential for more damage and loss of human life than could be achieved by our combined nuclear arsenals. Some even say that when conventional weapons are used during this conflict, they are likely to be our own turned against ourselves.

Via complex cyber intrusions, hacktivists have demonstrated their ability, from halfway around the world, to hack into an automobile's onboard computer, take control of the steering, brakes and acceleration, and run the car into a ditch, while the driver tried desperately to regain control in vain.

The same technological discoveries that created the framework of an automobile's control system pervade every aspect of our military hardware. To expect our military to have some magic that the auto manufacturers do not have, especially in the light of the recent Office of Personnel Management cyber intrusion referenced earlier in which tens of millions of private, and sometimes classified, personnel files were easily stolen by the Chinese and Russians, is absurd.

The world, and America in particular is on the edge of a steep cliff, about to be pushed over by any number of bad actors who would do us harm. Many believe our government is naïve—largely in denial at the greatest threat to America that has ever existed. The ostrich theory clearly applies, and the nation is at significant risk.

Advanced nations of the world have placed a great emphasis on cyber technologies and have left Americans behind. This same illiteracy does not exist in Russia, India, China, and Japan where advanced sciences take a priority during a student's formative years. Our lack of knowledge is also found in our nation's political leadership. In America, the threat of cyber warfare takes a back seat to social issues. In countries like China, Japan, and Russia, it's difficult to reach any level of political power without a vast knowledge of computer related technology.

To these countries, the concept of a government official who was not highly competent in the cyber sciences would be the equivalent of us having a president who could not read or write. This must drastically change and an increasing number of policy analysts believe we must accept cyber attacks from adversarial nation-states for what they are—acts of war—and respond accordingly.

Strides within the political hierarchy of this nation are being made in recent years. In November of 2011, the US government declared that it has the right to meet cyber attacks with military force. Although this is just a broad declaration, it's significant because it takes the first step towards a declaratory policy for cyber war. The policy statement provided, in essence: *We reserve our right to defend ourselves with bullets, missiles, and bombs in the event that you hack us*. The statement was vague and didn't mean much but fell short of drawing the line in the sand.

The Five Pillars

In 2010, United States Deputy Defense Secretary William Lynn introduced to the North Atlantic Treaty Organization (NATO) the framework for the United States military strategy for cyber warfare. Known as *The Five Pillars*, this cyber shield would extend a blanket of security over NATO member's networks similar to the nuclear defense shield.

Article 5 of the NATO charter states *an armed attacked on one of its members should be considered as an attack on all the members.* After the September 11 attacks, this article was invoked in dealing with global terrorism. With the rise in cyber terrorism and crimes, there might be a need to accommodate the cyber attacks in the enforcement of Article 5.

The first pillar is to recognize that the new domain for warfare is cyberspace similar to the other elements of the traditional battlefield.

The second pillar is the implementation of proactive defenses as opposed to relying on passive defenses. Two examples of passive defense are computer hygiene and firewalls. The balance of the attacks requires active defense using sensors to provide a rapid response in detecting and stopping a cyber attack on a computer network. This would provide military tactics to backtrace, hunt down and attack an offending enemy intruder.

The third pillar is critical infrastructure protection to ensure the security of power grids, transportation, communications, and financial sectors.

The fourth pillar is the use of collective defense involving both the public and private sectors, which would provide the ability of early detection and to incorporate them into the cyber warfare defense structure.

The fifth pillar is to actively maintain and enhance the advantage of technological change. This would include improved computer literacy and increasing artificial intelligence capabilities.

Are new Geneva conventions needed?

In 2015, members of the House Intelligence Committee urged fellow intelligence community leaders to help create international rules of engagement, similar to the Geneva Conventions, for cyber warfare.

"We don't know what constitutes an act of war, what the appropriate response is, what the line is between crime and warfare," said Connecticut Congressman Jim Himes at a committee hearing on global cyber threats. While Congressman Himes put the burden on Congress to push for such international norms, he suggested that the nation's intelligence agencies have neglected to create a clear set of standards. Rep. Adam Schiff (Calif.), the ranking Democrat on the committee and Himes, have rung the clarion bell and argue some high-level policy questions about how the U.S. treats cyberspace are still unanswered.

Experts agree there are three distinct kinds of cyber intrusions:

- economic spying in cyberspace which is intended to benefit foreign companies financially;

- cyber attacks designed to do damage to critical infrastructure and utilities, and

- traditional intelligence-gathering efforts performed by nation-states.

"For many of our adversaries in this realm, like the Chinese, there's a benefit to blurring the distinctions here," Congressman Schiff said in an interview with The Hill. "If they can blur the distinctions, they can justify anything they do. It seems to me it's in our best interest to draw a line between economic espionage and intelligence gathering. Shouldn't we make clear what the rules of the road are?"

But how should the United States, and perhaps its NATO allies, treat the various kinds of cyber activity? At what point would the theft of classified information constitute an act of war? At what point would a cyber attack result in a military or economic response beyond cyberspace?

Director of National Intelligence James Clapper and National Security Agency Director Michael Rogers pushed back on placing too much responsibility on the intelligence community to create international standards, characterizing such rulemaking as high-level policy decisions.

"The application of cyber in an offensive way is an application of force," Rogers said. "In the broad policy context we use as nations, it will be a decision is made at a broad policy level. That's not a decision I unilaterally decide."

On a policy level, the adaptation of a set of international standards is attainable as it provides other nation-states some understanding of how the U.S. will respond to cyber intrusions. It would, in theory, have a significant deterrent effect. The United States should take the lead in establishing a roadmap, recognized internationally, on how cyber warfare and cyber criminal activity will be dealt with between countries. Some suggest that such norms will evolve over time. The question has to be asked—cyber attacks can happen so quickly, will the standards come too late?

Chapter Eight
The Problem of Attribution

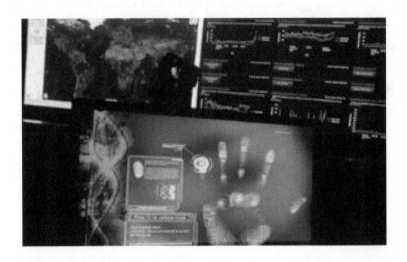

Attribution—or lack thereof—is another major obstacle that prevents nations from defining when a bad actor can start a war via cyber attack. If a government cannot determine who carried out the attack, it's difficult to know who to blame and whether the attack warrants a response. Without definitive evidence leading to identification of the intruder, a state can't formulate an appropriate response without knowing who was involved. This challenge is on clear display with the Sony attack. At various times, investigators have attributed the attacks to North Korea, China, and even Sony employees. The FBI, after initially saying there was no connection between North Korea and the attack, has since concluded that indeed North Korea did carry out the attack—a conclusion that led to U.S. sanctions against the secluded country. For a time, it was alleged a disgruntled employee was behind the cyber intrusion—or perhaps both working in concert.

Just like any criminal investigation, if law enforcement could somehow figure out the assailant, then a lot of issues go away. If you know who's conducting the cyber activity, you also get an insight into their intent. If it's the Russian government, you know they have the ability to take things a step further. If it's some hacker in his mom's basement, you know there's no intent or ability to raise the level of force that's going to be used. Ultimately, the issue of attribution is not a legal problem; it's a technical problem.

Determining whether a non-state entity is acting under the direction of the state further complicates the attribution problem. If it turns out that the Sony attack can't be tied directly to the North Korea government, but rather to a group of non-state-affiliated individuals—North Korea's response would be these individuals were just *patriots*. What level of command-and-control or even sponsorship is required before a state is held accountable for the cyber activity?

The problem of attribution won't soon be solved. Most of the cyber attacks undertaken will require patient waiting and watching to establish a pattern. One policy analyst summarized the approach as follows: "We watch what states do over time and it sort of settles. State takes an action, no one objects, or everyone objects. We have a lot of people who want answers right now, but we're in for a period of uncertainty."

Attribution, the process of detecting an adversaries fingerprints on a cyber attack, will always be a challenge. Establishing any degree of confidence in determining guilt may always stand in the way of a military response. Will the United States government require a *beyond all reasonable doubt standard* as it might in a criminal prosecution? Time will tell.

CHAPTER NINE
U. S. DEPARTMENT OF DEFENSE
PREPARATIONS

United States Cyber Command (USCYBERCOM) is an armed forces sub-unified command subordinate to United States Strategic Command. The command is located at Fort Meade, Maryland, and centralizes command of cyberspace operations, organizes existing cyber resources and synchronizes defense of U.S. military networks. USCYBERCOM synchronizes and conducts activities to direct the operations and defense of specified Department of Defense information networks, The agency also conducts full-spectrum military cyberspace operations in order to enable actions in all domains, ensure US/Allied freedom of action in cyberspace and deny the same to our adversaries. USCYBERCOM is charged with pulling together existing cyberspace resources, creating synergy and synchronizing war-fighting effects to defend the information security environment.

The Department of Homeland Security's United States Computer Emergency Readiness Team (US-CERT) is the 24-hour operational arm of the Department of Homeland Security's National Cybersecurity and Communications Integration Center. This team leads efforts to improve the Nation's cybersecurity posture, coordinate cyber information sharing, and proactively manage cyber risks to American interests. US-CERT strives to be a trusted global leader in cyber security—collaborative, agile, and responsive in a dynamic and complex environment. The government partners with private sector critical infrastructure operators, and domestic and international organizations to enhance the nation's cybersecurity posture.

In 2015, the U.S. took an important step designed to deter potential cyber adversaries when it released a new strategy that for the first time explicitly discusses the circumstances under which cyber weapons could be used against an attacker. Further, the Pentagon named the countries it says present the greatest threat: China, Russia, Iran, North Korea, and, for the first time, ISIS.

Defense Secretary Ash Carter announced the new policy in a speech at Stanford University, representing the fourth time in a period of four months during 2015 that the Obama administration has specifically named nation-states as being responsible for cyber activity detrimental to the U.S. The speech further announced new strategies designed to raise the geopolitical cost of conducting cyber attacks.

The administration's previous strategy was less detailed and only suggested there was a new arsenal of cyber weapons available to the Pentagon in cyber warfare. The 2011 policy did not name any specific offenders.

President Obama's decision to publicly declare North Korea's leaders guilty of ordering the cyber attack on Sony Pictures, the largest destructive attack on any American target, public or private, was welcomed by cyber security specialists. The availability of new sanctions against state-sponsored and criminal hackers, and the subsequent indictment of five members of the People's Liberation Army by the U.S. Justice Department for attacking American business interests all reflected a substantial change in Washington's policy.

American officials have fumed for years that cyber attacks were allowed without retribution. In the middle of the twentieth century, as nuclear weapons gained favor as a military option, Presidents Truman and Eisenhower struggled to define circumstances that could prompt a nuclear response from Washington. Now, the President's policy advisors are beginning to lay out conditions under which USCYBERCOM would employ cyber counter-attacks — including in retaliation for a previous cyber attacks, as an offensive weapon for conflict or in covert action.

In his speech at Stanford, Mr. Carter revealed that the Pentagon, as did the White House and the State Department, found itself the victim of a cyber attack in 2015. He stated, "The sensors that guard DoD's unclassified networks detected Russian hackers are accessing one of our networks." He further said the attack exploited "an old vulnerability in one of our legacy networks that hadn't been patched." This is very typical of the vulnerabilities used by hackers on private sector networks. Obviously, our government's networks are every bit as vulnerable.

Obama administration officials would not say if the cyber attacks mentioned by Secretary Carter bore similarities to attacks on the White House and the State Department during 2014. Those attacks, which also appeared to be of Russian origin, were kept under wraps for many months following the incident. Until Carter's speech at Stanford, the administration had not named an adversary.

One of the purposes of Carter's high-profile speech was the introduction of the core of a new cyber strategy published by the Pentagon identifying a hierarchy of cyber attacks. The administration's new strategy stated routine attacks and cyber vandalism should be fended off by private sector companies without the assistance of the government. The Department of Homeland Security will assist in detecting more sophisticated attacks and helping the private sector defend against them.

But, in a significant declaration, certain attacks on American computer network systems may rise to the level of prompting a national response — led by the Pentagon and through the military's Cyber Command. Carter indicated that this may apply to a small percentage of cyber activity, but the event may be so severe a U.S. governmental response is necessary.

The administration's new strategy provides, in part: "as a matter of principle, the United States will seek to exhaust all network defense and law enforcement options to mitigate any potential cyber risk to the U.S. homeland or U.S. interests before conducting a cyberspace operation.".

But it also opens the door for pre-emptive cyber attacks: "there may be times when the president or the secretary of defense may determine that it would be appropriate for the U.S. military to conduct cyber operations to disrupt an adversary's military related networks or infrastructure so that the U.S. military can protect U.S. interests in an area of operations. For example, the United States military might use cyber operations to terminate an ongoing conflict on U.S. terms, or to disrupt an adversary's military systems to prevent the use of force against U.S. interests."

Until now, most American cyber attacks on adversaries have been covert operations. It now appears something that threatens the significant loss of life, destruction of property or lasting economic damage could be responded to in kind, or militarily. That could cover many types of cyber attacks, but, by way of recent example, in the biggest case to date involving the private sector, the attack on Sony, the president chose to respond with sanctions on North Korea, and not in cyberspace.

Finally, at the heart of the diplomatic, economic and threatened military responses available to the U.S. Department of Defense is the concept of deterrence — something that the United States had a far easier time establishing in the nuclear arena than it has had in cyberspace, where it 's hard to establish attribution.

Deterrence is partially a function of perception most cyber security professionals say. Just like in conventional modern warfare, deterrence works by convincing a potential adversary that it will suffer unacceptable costs if it conducts an attack on the United States, thus decreasing the likelihood a potential adversary's attack will succeed. The United States must be able to declare or display adequate response capabilities to deter an adversary from initiating an attack; develop effective defensive capabilities to deny a potential attack from succeeding; and strengthen the overall resilience of U.S. systems to withstand a possible attack if it penetrates the United States' defenses.

But as Mr. Carter acknowledged in his Stanford speech, such a policy is easier to declare than to make vivid. The head of Cyber Command, Adm. Rogers, has often stated that the price of conducting cyber attacks is simply too low for many countries to resist.

Welcome to the world of asymmetric warfare—where the playing field is level for all.

CHAPTER TEN
RETALIATION – CYBER
COUNTER-TERRORISM

The NATO Position on Retaliation

NATO formed the Cooperative Cyber Defense Centre of Excellence (CCDCOE) which published a guideline of rules on how to respond to cyber aggression against the government. Among the intriguing possibilities of the guide—known as the Tallinn Manual, is it suggests the United States and its European allies have the option to retaliate against cyber attacks from domestic hackers.

The NATO Cyber War Manual deals with the many controversial issues including the identification and attribution of civilian attackers.

The manual was written over the course of three years by a team of 20 international warfare experts and drew from a variety of historic warfare guidelines, including the 1868 St. Petersburg Declaration and the 1949 Geneva Convention. These principles were then applied to the digital world.

It suggests that *hacktivists* can be considered cyber terrorists, thus eligible for a like-kind digital response in retaliation. In extreme cases, such as attacks on hospitals or nuclear plants, physical force is an available option by the NATO alliance.

The rulebook was unveiled at the Chatham House in London. It contains 95 *black letter rules* spread over 302 pages of text. Colonel Kirby Abbott, representing Canadian interests at NATO remarked, "The Tallinn Manual is the most important document in the rules of cyber warfare. It will be highly useful."

Among the most relevant provisions is rule twenty-two that echoes previous cyber warfare guidelines from the Pentagon stating cyber attacks alone can be considered acts of war. It reads, in part:

An international armed conflict exists whenever there are hostilities, which may include or be limited to cyber operations occurring between two states or more.

To date, no international armed conflict has been precipitated by the use of cyber warfare. Nevertheless, the international group of experts unanimously concluded that cyber operations alone might have the potential to cross the threshold allowing international armed conflict.

Another important aspect of the Tallinn Manual is rule fourteen in which the concept of proportionality is addressed. The document suggests that cyber retaliation against civilians is allowed although unspecified, general attacks on civilian targets are generally forbidden. The proportionality rule suggests that if hacktivist attacks cause death or serious harm, a physical response (e.g. a drone death strike) may be acceptable.

Does the Tallinn Manual open the door for counterattacks on the hacktivist group Anonymous?

The rules raise a number of interesting scenarios.

In recent years, Anonymous and other *hacktivist* groups have caused substantial damage to the networks and reputation of the United States government. They have defaced U.S. government web pages, acquired sensitive government data via cyber intrusions, hit government domains with distributed denial of service attacks, infiltrated network systems, and conducted similar attacks on government contractors as well.

The glossary of the Tallinn Manual defines a *hacktivist* as:

A private citizen who on his or her own initiative engages in hacking for, among other things, ideological, political, religious or patriotic reasons.

Rule thirty-five goes further and establishes rules related to attacks by *hacktivist* civilians. It reads:

An act of direct participation in hostilities by civilians renders them liable to be attacked, by cyber or other lawful means.

In other words, the NATO members agreed that civilians open themselves up to counterattacks if they attack NATO member-state governments. However, not all members agreed that this opens up those citizens for attacks in the long-term after the immediate threat passed. Some member-states draw the line once the immediate danger of cyber terrorism is over.

As none of these attacks caused *significant* infrastructure damage or resulted in death, it seems the NATO allies, under the new rules, would only be able to use digital counterattacks. However, the government could potentially use the rules as a justification to shut down social media tools utilized by hacktivist groups like Anonymous.

If future attacks resulted in death as a consequence of an attack on the power grid, the responsible civilians could face physical attacks. This could potentially include the kind of drone death strikes the Obama administration has used liberally throughout the world.

Might the U.S. be allowed to initiate counter cyber attacks against China?

The U.S. government has increasingly accused China of sweeping government-endorsed hacking and intellectual property theft.

President Obama recently threatened economic *consequences* if the cyber intrusions continue. The Tallinn Manual would address the Chinese use of cyber attacks in rule seven. Rule seven states when there is insufficient evidence of a suspected attack originating from a government network, a victim state may attribute the operation to that state where there is an indication that the state in question is associated with the operation.

This could be significant, as some attacks have reportedly been traced back to Chinese military networks. The new guidelines make it clear that the U.S. Department of Defense's USCYBERCOM could also respond in kind with counterattacks, as the guidelines state that cyber attacks on hostile foreign governments are valid if carried out in self-defense.

Lastly, based upon the new guidelines, and the historical use of cyber attacks by the United States, was the Stuxnet attack on Iranian nuclear facilities legal?

The guidelines revive questions about the legality of the U.S. and Israel's *pre-emptive* strike on Iran's nuclear capabilities with Stuxnet. If the Pentagon's rules, and now NATO's rules, call cyber attacks an act of war, the question is whether the past two administrations were within the law in ordering the Stuxnet operation.

Article 1, Section 8 of the U.S. Constitution, the foundation of the U.S. government, clearly grants Congress the power:

The Congress shall have Power To lay and collect Taxes, Duties, Imposts and Excises, to pay the Debts and provide for the common Defence and general Welfare of the United States; but all Duties, Imposts and Excises shall be uniform throughout the United States;

To raise and support armies, but no appropriation of money to that use shall be for a longer term than two years.

Article 1 typically required the President to receive Congressional permission to go to war. This section of the constitution has been abandoned somewhat as the Executive Branch uses semantics to circumvent its requirements.

In summary, the new manual adopted by NATO is simply a suggested guideline for NATO members but is not considered an accepted rule of law. NATO has no power to enforce its provisions, although member states are encouraged to do so. It should be noted that the document is rather ambiguous in its language at times, and at others makes it clear that the participating member states did not agree on a number of issues. If the Tallinn Manual does not have the force and effect of law and is just considered a guideline, then:

How does a victim state respond to a state-sponsored cyber attack?

As cyber terrorism and cyber vandalism become more prevalent, policymakers will be challenged to develop appropriate responses to destructive cyber intrusions. As the quantity and intensity of cyber intrusions have increased, governments have been placed under significant pressure to retaliate. Raising public awareness in light of the allegedly state-sponsored attacks on Sony Pictures and the Sands Casino has helped bring the issue to the forefront. But finding an opportune, proportionate, legal, and acceptable response is complicated by the difficulty in assessing the damage to national interests and the frequent use of state sponsored hacktivists. Most nation-states have plausible deniability, frustrating efforts to declare attribution. Experience suggests that most policy responses have been ad hoc.

In determining the measured response to a state-sponsored cyber intrusion, policymakers will need to consider three important factors—the intelligence community's confidence in its determination of responsibility, the economic or physical impact of the cyber attack, and the options available to the victim.

While these factors will help create an appropriate response to a disruptive or destructive cyber attack, policymakers will also need to consider additional steps before responding. First, policymakers will need to work with the private sector to determine the effect of an incident on their operations. Second, governments should publicly announce a series of preplanned response options to act as a deterrent while being cognizant of the potential impact of any response on political, economic, intelligence, and military interests.

As the number of highly disruptive and destructive cyber attacks grows, governments remain uncertain as to an appropriate response. In non-digital national security matters, policy responses to the state-sponsored activity are well defined. The government can expel diplomats in response to a spying scandal and use force in response to an armed attack. Clear and established policy responses such as these do not yet exist for cyber attacks for two reasons.

First, assessing the damage caused by a cyber incident is a time-consuming, complicated process. It can take weeks, if not months, for computer forensic experts to accurately and conclusively ascertain the extent of the damage done to an organization's computer networks. For example, it took roughly two weeks for Saudi authorities, with the assistance of the FBI, to understand the extent of the damage of the ARAMCO incident, which erased data on thirty thousand of Saudi Aramco's computers. Although this may be quick by computer forensics standards, by comparison, the military can conduct a damage assessment from a non-cyber incident in as little as a few hours.

Second, attributing cyber intrusions to their state-sponsor will always be a significant challenge. Masking the true origins of a cyber attack is relatively easy. States often use proxies or compromised computers in other jurisdictions to divert attention from the real attacker. For example, when the group calling itself the Cyber Caliphate claimed responsibility for taking French television station TV5 Monde off the air with a cyber attack in April 2015, it used the television station's own social media accounts to post content in support of the self-proclaimed Islamic State. French media reported two weeks later that Russian state-sponsored actors, not pro–Islamic State groups as originally alleged, were likely behind the incident. Even when attribution is determined, it is not guaranteed that domestic or foreign audiences will believe the claim unless officials reveal potentially classified methods used to ascertain the identity of the perpetrator. Disclosure of the attacker could potentially damage intelligence assets. Under the increased public awareness and pressure associated with cyber attacks, responses are likely to be made quickly with incomplete evidence and will attract a high degree of public skepticism. This creates substantial exposure for policymakers who rush to judgment. Quick damage assessments could lead to an overestimation of the impact of an incident, causing a state to respond disproportionately. Misattributing an incident could cause a response to be directed at the wrong target, creating a diplomatic crisis.

Applying traditional analysis in the military world to the new digital one, governments should consider three aspects of the cyber attack before developing an appropriate response.

First, they should understand the level of confidence that their intelligence agencies have in attributing the incident. Digital forensics is not perfect, although there have been great strides in intelligence agencies' ability to attribute malicious activity. The degree of certainty must have a direct impact on the action taken. For example, if the level of attribution is low, policymakers will be limited in their choice of response even if the severity of the attack is high. They may choose a less valuable retaliatory target to limit the odds of escalation and international criticism. There may also be instances where there is so little evidence for the source of the attack that the victim may choose not to respond.

Second, policymakers should assess the cyber incident's effects on physical infrastructure, society, the economy, and national interests. The answers to these questions will significantly impact the level of response. Several inquiries come to mind. *What was the physical damage caused by the cyber intrusion? Was there any impact on critical infrastructure? What type of essential services is affected? Has the incident caused significant economic loss or loss of confidence in the markets? What was the incident's impact on national security and the country's reputation?*

Third, policymakers should consider the range of diplomatic, economic, and military responses at their disposal, from a quiet diplomatic rebuke to a military strike. As the guidelines outlined in the Tallinn Manual submitted to NATO, responses need not be limited to cyberspace. Depending upon the answers to the questions above, nothing bars a state from using other options, although each carries its risks, as is always the case when responding to an attack—military or digital.

Cyber responses can be taken in addition to diplomatic, economic, and military activity. However, they would most often be delivered covertly and could be difficult to develop quickly. The responses would likely involve cyber espionage, after an assessment of a target's vulnerabilities, and a custom exploit attack designed to implement the measured response. As an example, Stuxnet reportedly took years to develop and deploy. Although states may outsource their retaliation to a proxy, doing so could limit their control over the response and lead to an escalation of activity. Therefore, policymakers are likely to concentrate on other levers of power, outside the cyber realm, in addition to what they may do covertly via cyber tools.

Given the likely pressure governments will feel to respond to significant cyber attacks, policymakers need to develop a response framework before a disruptive or destructive cyber incident occurs. Although each response will be case specific, a structure will enable policymakers to consider their options quickly.

As with other areas of international relations, proportionality emerges through state practice. When one country levies economic sanctions, the sanctioned country often responds in kind. For example, Russia responded to U.S. sanctions over its annexation of Crimea with sanctions of its own. This same logic applies to cyberspace. While there may be pressure to respond aggresively to deter future attacks, accepted international standards require that states only take forcible measures necessary and proportionate to repel or defeat a destructive cyber attack successfully. International law limits the scale, scope, duration and intensity of any actions a victim state may take. Furthermore, a proportional response may pave the way for international coalition building, encouraging the isolation and punishment of the attacker while avoiding the likelihood of escalation.

If a country is the victim of state-sponsored website defacement, a public denouncement is likely the most appropriate response. Moving up the scale, any activity that begins to manipulate or destroy data would potentially require diplomatic action, such as the traditional expulsion of diplomats if the incident affects the victim's economy. Once the economy is adversely affected, a range of economic responses can be used in coordination with diplomatic pressure, from freezing financial transactions by the sponsoring nation-state to levying international sanctions. Should an incident cause physical damage, a policymaker could consider a military option as an appropriate and proportional response, from military posturing to attack, depending on the incident's severity. All of these options can be complemented with cyber or covert action, which should also be proportionate to the damage caused by the incident to gain international acceptance.

The United States should begin developing its policy response framework by first working with the private sector, particularly in critical infrastructure. Our nation's power grid is a priority for attackers, making it important for infrastructure operators to be involved in the development of a framework. The nation's utilities should advise the government on incidents that affect their operations and report the severity of any incident before a response is formulated.

The growing threat of cyber warfare provides nation-states with a complex set of decisions to make—from understanding the severity of the incident to assessing appropriate responses to take, while continually evaluating the risks involved in formulating a response. As the threats to our nation grow, our government needs to address these issues in depth.

PART FIVE

CYBER ATTACKS AS ACTS OF WAR

CHAPTER ELEVEN
DOES CYBER VANDALISM FALL SHORT OF AN ACT OF WAR?

Military and national security operations in cyberspace have made headlines with increasing frequency.

Security companies for several years have documented massive cyber-espionage by the Chinese military against the United States—both private and public sectors. As discussed, the Department of Justice responded by indicting five Chinese military officers for computer hacking, economic espionage, and other offenses directed at American nuclear power, metals, and solar products companies.

Snowden's allegations of massive cyber spying by the National Security Agency and close American allies have raised worldwide fears about the security and privacy of the Internet.

Russia and Iran have been accused of launching covert cyber espionage against political and economic targets in the U.S. According to reports, it appears Russian hackers attempted to place a *digital bomb* inside the NASDAQ stock exchange networks.

Fears are growing that, similar to the outbreak of World War I a century ago, a cyber event—the equivalent of the Serbian gunman's assassination of the Austro-Hungarian Duke in Sarajevo—could escalate into an outright cyber war with dire consequences around the world.

Cyber warfare is one of the most misused terms in the cyber dictionary. The U.S. Strategic Command defines cyber warfare as: *The Creation of effects in and through cyberspace in support of a combatant commander's military objectives, to ensure friendly forces freedom of action in cyberspace while denying adversaries these same freedoms.*

There are traditional definitions as to what constitutes an act of war, and the cyber version is only slightly different. Cyber warfare has been defined as an action, or series of actions, by a military commander or government-sponsored cyber warriors that further his or her objectives, while disallowing an enemy to achieve theirs. Military leaders typically belong to a nation-state or a well-funded, overt and organized insurgency group (as opposed to loosely organized rebels, crime syndicates, etc.). Acting overtly in cyberspace means you are not trying to hide who you are, although it's relatively easy to mask your tracks. The warriors of today are the cyber version of regular, uniformed forces versus irregular forces.

In 2014, Sony executives, gearing up for the release of Seth Rogen's North Korea-bashing film, The Interview, received an ominous holiday greeting—"*We've obtained all your internal data including your secrets and top secrets. If you don't obey us, we'll release data shown below to the world.*" The hackers delivered on their promise, unloading onto the internet an incredible number of emails, employee information, and all sorts of other data. Most of the actual damage involved disclosed personnel records and damaged celebrity reputations. Among other things, producer Mark Rudin called Angelina Jolie *a minimally talented spoiled brat* for delaying his film projects, and producer Amy Pascal called Leonardo DiCaprio *absolutely despicable* after he passed on a Steve Jobs biopic.

A few politicians focused on the Sony cyber attack's political and economic implications. "It's a new form of warfare that we're involved in," Senator John McCain told CNN's State of the Union, "and we need to react and we need to react vigorously." Senator McCain's condemnation was in large part a response to President Obama's earlier acknowledgment that, while indeed an act of *cyber vandalism*, the Sony cyber attack doesn't quite qualify as an act of war. Congressman Mike Rogers, the Republican chair of the House Intelligence Committee, was more reserved in his assessment. "You can't necessarily say an act of war," he expressed in an interview with Fox News. Rogers identified the underlying legal problem when he admitted, "We don't have good, clear policy guidance on what that means when it comes to cyber attacks."

Was the cyber attack on Sony cyber—vandalism, warfare, or something else? If the Sony cyber attack didn't cross the line into cyber warfare, what would?

After President Obama stated that the Sony hack was an act of cyber vandalism perpetrated by North Korea—and thus not an act of war, the statement was criticized by politicians, security experts and other members of the public. Before a rush to judgment is made, one must look at what constitutes an act of war. Let's assume for the sake of this analysis that North Korea did perpetrate the attack. Was the act part of a military maneuver, directed by a commander, with the purpose of denying the enemy freedom of action while providing a tactical advantage on its end? No. The objective was to embarrass a private-sector firm and degrade or deny computing services. Under this analysis, the President is right – it's clearly not part of a military operation. It's on the extreme end of vandalism, but that's all it is.

Few public examples exist of true, overt cyber warfare. Allegations have been made that the U.S., Israel, Russia, China, and Iran have engaged in cyber war at some point, but the accounts either use a looser definition of cyber war.

One of the early candidates for a textbook example of cyber war occurred during the 2008 Russo-Georgian War. Russia and Georgia engaged in armed conflict with two breakaway republics, South Ossetia and Abkhazia – both located in Georgia. Russia backed the separatists and eventually launched a military campaign. In the days and weeks leading up to Russia's direct military intervention, hackers originating from within Russia attacked key Georgian information assets. Internet connectivity was down for extended periods of time and official government websites were hacked or completely under the attacker's control. In addition, internal communications and news outlets were severely disrupted. All of the above would hamper the ability of Georgian military commanders to coordinate defenses during the initial Russian land attack.

Considering the Sony attack as a typical example, or perhaps a cyber attack that causes a financial market crash but, because it does not directly harm people or the infrastructure necessary for preserving life and health, doesn't meet criteria for a conventional act of war. By accepted definitions of warfare, this may not constitute an act of war against the United States—and thus only cyber vandalism, but the affected companies might disagree.

CHAPTER TWELVE
WHEN IS IT AN ACT OF WAR?
WHAT IS AN APPROPRIATE RESPONSE?

In 2012, former Defense Secretary Leon Panetta stood inside the Intrepid Sea, Air and Space Museum moored in New York and addressed an audience of business executives. He informed them of one of the most important conversations being held inside the corridors of the United States government.

Pearl Harbor was one of the most tragic moments in American history. Japanese bombers unleashed a devastating surprise attack on a U.S. naval base in Hawaii on that seventh day of December in 1941, killing twenty-four hundred Americans and wounding another thirteen hundred. President Franklin D. Roosevelt called it *a date that will live in infamy* during his speech asking Congress for a declaration of war.

Sixty years later, another surprise attack killed almost three thousand people when Muslim terrorists flew two airplanes into New York's World Trade Center towers and the Pentagon. Panetta referenced the September 11, 2001, strikes, warning that the United States is in a *pre-9/11 moment*, with critical computer systems vulnerable to assault.

He told the businessmen that America is vulnerable to a *cyber Pearl Harbor.*

An act of war by military means is apparent. By mentioning two of the most egregious attacks in U.S. history, Panetta effectively raised a sense of urgency about the threat in the cyber domain.

But when does a cyber attack give rise to an act of war?

Panetta called the Saudi Aramco assault, along with a similar strike on Qatar's RasGas, *probably the most destructive attack* on the private sector to date. These highly destructive attacks crossed the line from cyber vandalism to cyber war said one U.S. official, who declared it a *watershed moment* in the new age of digital warfare. Attacks on critical infrastructure go beyond the troubling—but all-too-familiar—thefts of data and disruption of Web sites. They threaten the lives of human beings, especially the vulnerable.

Unlike the Japanese planes at Pearl Harbor, the cyber attacks on ARAMCO and RasGas had no visible digital footprints that gave away its origins. Privately, sources in the intelligence community believe the invader was sponsored by Iran.

If the Iranians are responsible, what was the motive? In the view of some pundits, Iran was striking back for sanctions imposed upon it with the complicity of the Saudi kingdom's support for an oil embargo. Another theory surrounded the damage done to Iran's nuclear program by Stuxnet, which slowed the country's pursuit of a nuclear weapon by destroying nearly one thousand uranium-enrichment centrifuges.

The Shamoon attack on Saudi Aramco did not cause enough physical damage to rise to what international law experts call an armed assault—thus an act of war. Consider this. What if something like it happened to Exxon, Shell and BP operations in the United States? What if it could be traced conclusively to a foreign government or a terrorist group? How much damage, pain, and fear would need to result before administration officials would say, "This is an act of war"?

There does not seem to be a definitive agreement by the State Department and Pentagon officials on this issue. Japan's attack on Pearl Harbor was a direct assault on a U.S. military installation—clearly, an act of war. But much of the nation's critical infrastructure networks belong to the private sector. Companies that provide transportation, water, telecommunications, and energy could become targets for adversaries determined to put America in the dark. That simple fact has led to a complicated set of questions for policymakers responsible for the nation's security.

Should the U.S. government step in to prevent a destructive cyber attack upon privately owned and operated utilities? Assuming the cyber terrorism can be conclusively traced to another nation or a terrorist group, when should the U.S. retaliate and to what extent? Under what circumstances should our government make pre-emptive use of cyber weapons to alter a nation-state's agenda or behavior?

By way of example, if a significant cyber attack is initiated, such as a virus knocking out air traffic control and wreaking havoc on the airline system, what would be the appropriate response of our government? It is likely the President and the National Security Council would focus first on what type of reply would be proportionate, justified, and necessary and in the U.S. interest. It might be a military response. It might be retaliation in cyber space. It might be the exposure of the attacker before the United Nations, demanding the imposition of sanctions. With the problems of attribution, it might be no response at all.

Deciding what amounts to an act of war is more a political judgment than a military or legal one. General James Cartwright, former vice chairman of the Joint Chiefs of Staff, was quoted as saying *an act of war is in the eye of the beholder*. Typically, an act of war requires international consensus.

If the United States didn't go to war with North Korea after it sank a South Korean warship in 2010, nor with Iran after the U.S. Embassy in Tehran was seized in 1979, would the American people accept a war over a power outage? The administration has defined an armed attack in cyberspace as one that results in death, injury or significant destruction. Here's the rule of thumb as expressed by policymakers:

If the physical consequences of a cyber attack work the kind of physical damage that dropping a bomb or firing a missile would, that cyber attack should equally be considered a use of force. If an attack reaches those levels, then a nation has a right to act in *self-defense.*

The more severe cases will look something like what happened to Saudi Aramco, Ashley Madison's website and Sony Pictures. Economic damage or embarrassment alone does not give rise to a right of self-defense in the form of a military response. Those instances are certainly not worthy of an armed response, although the affected companies might disagree.

A more complicated scenario—a cyber attack on Wall Street computers that sends the markets into a tailspin and causes ripple effects throughout the economy, might generate sufficient economic damage on the nation's economy to warrant a more severe response. Although such an attack would be difficult to implement, it is one of those low-probability, high consequence events that cyber experts fear.

In the United States, senior policymakers have been wrestling with these very issues. The Saudi Aramco and Sony Picture attacks have raised awareness and the sense of urgency, making the cyber threat all the more plausible. As one U.S. intelligence official was reported as saying, "this was a deliberately disruptive event, done on purpose, not by some rogue hacker. Not some out-of-control operative."

Panetta further elaborated on this in his speech, saying "If a crippling cyber attack were launched against our nation, the American people must be protected." But what is the definition of *crippling*? What exactly would the role of the military be? Perhaps we will know the results of those closed door discussions when the cyber attack occurs.

Apparently, officials have done a lot of work on how the government would respond to individual attacks. "We feel we're very prepared to answer that question if it should come up in the case of the United States," said one senior Pentagon official in a Washington Times interview. But he would not get into hypotheticals, such as whether a cyber attack that caused a drop in the stock market or a huge increase in gas prices would trigger a military response.

"Those are always classified things," he said. "It's not helpful for the United States to give the enemy our detailed position on whether something is an attack on the nation and when it is not."

Makes sense. Why tell other nations what the United States is willing to tolerate before it responds forcefully? One might argue deterrence. We have maintained a vast nuclear arsenal under the guise of deterrence. Why not show our hands to prevent an attack, rather than respond to one which has a devastating impact on our nation's infrastructure.

Toward that end, the U.S. and its allies may be moving toward a greater strategic use of cyber weapons to dissuade adversaries from using cyber attacks against them. This can be good if it averts war. On the other hand, it could cause other nations to feel vulnerable. Some experts foresee a potential cyber arms race as nation-states try to maintain an edge.

Some argue that the term *act of war* is a dated one. The use of the terminology—*act of war*—was a more common term when used in conjunction with an Article 1 declaration via Congress. But the Geneva Conventions of 1949 actually dispensed with the requirement that war be declared before the rules of war apply.

During any discussion of whether a cyber attack is an act of war, the following questions arise:

When is a cyber attack an unlawful *use of force* under the United Nations Charter?

When can the victim state respond with physical force because the cyber attack qualifies as an *armed attack* under the U.N. Charter?

While the difference is a matter of semantics and far more relevant to the rest of the world, Washington does not distinguish between the two. The Tallinn Manual addressed several factors:

•Severity: How much damage did the attack cause?

•Immediacy: How quickly the consequences of the attack manifest themselves.

•Directness: How many intermediate steps had to occur between the attack and the consequences?

•Invasiveness: How much security did the attack have to bypass to cause its results?

•Measurability of effects: How easy is it to measure the damage caused?

•Military involvement: How involved was the military in carrying out the attack?

•State involvement: How involved was the state in carrying out the attack?

•Presumptive legality: Was the attack more akin to a military act, or was it merely propaganda, espionage, or economic pressure?

On one end of the spectrum are acts that don't constitute acts of war, like espionage. On the other end are acts that do constitute a use of force—say, military aggression. It's a relatively simple process to determine whether an act constitutes military force and, accordingly, if the victim nation has the right to respond.

"If you have a cyber operation that causes physical damage or injuries to a person, that's an armed attack, and you can respond forcefully," proponents of the Tallinn Manual say. "When a cyber attack doesn't reach that threshold, things become more complicated. Everyone agrees that certain cyber operations are clearly not armed attacks, for example, cyber espionage." Under these parameters, shutting down the national economy is probably an act of war, but short of that, it's not certain. By example, the Sony attack would fall outside of the gray area and, therefore, did not constitute an act of war.

So when would a cyber attack constitute an act of war? Based upon the Tallinn Manual, the only cyber attack that could have constituted an armed attack was allegedly carried out by the U.S. and Israel—Stuxnet.

Instead of demanding retribution from the U.S. or Israel, Iran stayed quiet for two years—until the Saudi Aramco incident. As chronicled herein, while no physical damage resulted, it took Aramco several weeks to replace tens of thousands of hard drives to prevent further spread of the virus, causing significant disruption to the company. The next month, several significant attacks took down the websites of financial institutions in the U.S. and prevented bank customers from withdrawing funds. Both the Aramco attack and the financial system attacks were attributed to Iran. Even though two years separated the Stuxnet and Aramco/bank attacks, observers surmised that Iran was retaliating for the Stuxnet attacks.

Stuxnet is probably the closest thing we've had to an armed, physical attack. Stuxnet resulted in the physical destruction of the centrifuges. To achieve the same effect without the use of cyber tools, you would have had to go in and planted explosives or something similar to get that destructive behavior.

Stuxnet would have qualified as an armed attack, per the Tallinn Manual definition, and as discussed above, a cyber attack can be an armed attack where the effects are analogous to those that would result from an action otherwise qualifying as a kinetic armed attack. In other words, if a missile or bullet or explosive could have caused the damage—physical damage or personal injury—a cyber attack with the same result is an armed assault. Stuxnet, likely developed by the U.S. and Israel, met that test.

Despite Stuxnet qualifying as an armed attack, Iran never went to the United Nations Security Council to claim that the attack violated the U. N. charter's prohibition on the use of force. Iran could have done so and sought assistance to respond to the attack. In cyber warfare, victim states are reluctant to make that declaration. If you call it an *act of war*, and later your surrogates carry out the same sort of cyber attack in retaliation, you may establish a precedent you don't want to set. The response may be more than you bargained for.

CHAPTER THIRTEEN
IF THE U.S. GOVERNMENT DOESN'T
RESPOND, MIGHT THE COMPANY?

The next *world war* might not be a *war* at all.

The nature of cyber warfare – and whether the U.S. government would even be among the combatants – has become a daily discussion on news networks and within our government. Broadly speaking, the media and pundits are too quick to use the word *war* when it discusses harmful cyber activities.

If it's just theft, it's theft. If it's espionage, it's espionage. Neither theft nor espionage gives rise to an act of war.

War or not, increasing escalation is bound to produce some response, and as Washington struggles to defend the government from cyber intrusions, private companies have learned they cannot rely on protection from the government.

"Most companies have realized that the federal government is not coming to their rescue in the cyber sense," said one cyber security analyst. "They are essentially on their own against organized criminals in Russia, against state-sponsored hackers in China, against groups like Anonymous, and sort of the various threats out there that might be trying to steal their data or take out their systems."

Cyber security experts warn private sector companies not to strike back in the cybercrime sphere. Their theory is INTERPOL and the FBI already exists for the purpose of criminal investigations and, therefore, is fully aware that the cyber attack or vandalism is a crime. They suggest that the private sector shouldn't retaliate against adversaries. They would be, in essence, paying their employees to become criminals. That is the whole *two wrongs don't make it a right* theory.

If American firms start hacking foreign rivals in retribution, they'll be committing the same types of crimes perpetrated upon them.

But should private companies put their fortunes in the hands of law enforcement or the military? It all comes down to trust, the U.S. Department of Justice representatives argue, and sharing information with law enforcement is the best method of bringing hackers and cyber terrorists to justice.

Many cyber analysts disagree. "Companies are not just going to keep taking this," one expert warned in an interview with CNBC. "If the government is saying to them, *we can't actually protect you, and we're not necessarily going to go on the offense for you*, I think it's only a matter of time before you see a company take matters into its hands and essentially go on the offense and take the fight back to the hackers."

Will that fight take the form of U.S. companies hacking foreign firms, or even hacking foreign governments, such as China? All sorts of combinations are possible. Websites like HackersList.com, HireTheHacker.com, and CryptoHacker.com enable corporate IT departments to reach out and secure a team of cyber mercenaries to do their bidding. Sometimes, a victim wants to exact revenge or justice on their terms.

PART SIX
IS A CYBER WAR A REALISTIC THREAT?

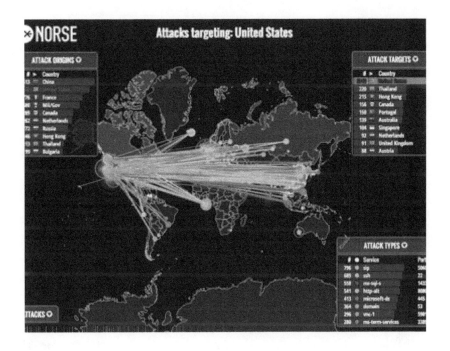

CHAPTER FOURTEEN
THE THREAT IS REAL

The very real threat posed to America by cyber warfare can be summarized by six central scenarios.

Over many decades, the U.S. has created the greatest military force the world has ever seen. But our research has proven that the biggest threat to national security comes from a computer with a simple Internet connection— not from aircraft carriers, tanks or drones. Having discussed the history of cyber warfare, its costs to both the private and public sectors, it's now time to address its increasingly important role in geopolitics.

Threats to the public sector.

The U.S. government has been fending off cyber attacks for years. The federal government fends off a staggering eighty thousand cyber attacks a year. The wave of hacks in 2014 exposed the records of over fourteen million current and former officials dating back to the mid-eighties. Compromised information includes Social Security numbers, fingerprints, military records, job assignments and medical histories. Clearly, this is dangerous information in the hands of our adversaries and the teams of cyber terrorists they employ. There is good reason DNI Clapper ranks cyber terrorism as the number one national security threat, ahead of traditional terrorism, espionage and weapons of mass destruction.

Threats to the private sector.

While rogue nation-states are interested in causing damage to governments, for some hackers and cyber criminals, cyber intrusions in the form of theft of intellectual property, personal data, and website defacement is enough to keep them occupied. The FBI notified nearly four thousand U.S. companies that they were the victims of cyber attacks in 2014. Victims of hackers ranged from the financial sector to major defense contractors to online retailers. Cyber security specialists report that almost ten percent of U.S. organizations lost $1 million dollars or more due to cybercrime in 2013 and another twenty percent of U.S. entities have claimed losses between $50,000 and $1 million over the same timeframe. According to the U.S, Chamber of Commerce, cyber attacks on the private sector costs the U.S. economy $300 billion per year. Some estimates claim that figure is closer to $445 billion, or a full 1 percent of global income, worldwide. It is projected that private firms around the world will spend $80 billion on cyber security in 2015 and that still won't be enough.

Use of social media to issue threats and calls to action for terrorists

Social media has become a haven for cyber criminals and terrorists. As Facebook, Twitter and Pinterest have become an integral part of our lives, criminals now use these venues to commit cyber theft or as a method of communication for terrorists. Nearly one in three U.S. adults say one of their social media accounts has been compromised. Cyber security analysts believe ten to fifteen percent of home computers globally are already infected with viruses and malware. We live in a society where your online social media presence increasingly defines you to the rest of the world. Enterprising hackers with access to your accounts can cause untold damage to both your personal and professional reputation. In 2011, Facebook openly admitted that it was the target of six hundred thousand cyber attacks daily. After the unexpected uproar over these numbers, and in an effort to avoid scaring off potential users, Facebook hasn't released official figures since. Vast terrorist networks have been established worldwide which use social media as a means to spread their doctrines to recruits or to issues calls to action for established members of their network. A recent attack on military recruiting centers in Tennessee was prompted by social media encouragement by ISIS.

Use of the cyber arena to spread propaganda to gain economic or military advantage

The Russians established a sophisticated propaganda machine under the supervision of its Internet Research Agency that waged a massive disinformation campaign in support for its annexation of Crimea and its invasion of Ukraine. These hired guns work hard, each one pumping out hundreds of comments and blog posts per shift. In addition, each hacktivist troll is reportedly required to post 50 news articles a day while maintaining half a dozen Facebook and more than ten Twitter accounts. It is not unusual for this machine to be used to gain a militaristic advantage as the Russians spread incorrect information throughout the online media.

Use of cyber attacks to conduct industrial espionage

While the Russians are notorious for gaining a military advantage through the use of cyber tactics, the Chinese are a determined bunch when comes to stealing valuable public and private sector trade secrets. The vast majority of America's intellectual property theft is believed to originate from China. The Chinese employ elite hackers housed by the government throughout the world to mask their real affiliations. China's goal has been to catch up with the U.S. in direct military strength. Washington already outspends China more than 4-to-1 in growing its military that makes achieving military parity very difficult. Rather than attempting to outspend the U.S., Beijing's answer has been to focus instead on commercial and government espionage. The Chinese computer spies employed by the PLA have attempted raids on the networks of almost every major U.S. defense contractor and have stolen some of our nation's most closely guarded technological secrets.

The biggest threat: Collapse of the nation's power grid

On July 8, 2015, Americans watched as trading was halted on the

New York Stock Exchange (NYSE) floor. At the same time, computer reservation systems at United Airlines were down, and the Wall Street Journal newspaper computer networks crashed.

This was not a scene from your favorite author's books of fiction; it was very real. According to reports, the interruption of the services mentioned was a mere *coincidence,* and the events were *unrelated.* These incidents and many more have raised public awareness of the vulnerability of our nation's critical infrastructure.

At the time, White House spokesperson Josh Earnest asserted the incidents weren't caused by cyber attacks, but were typical software issues that happened to coincide in time. However, he did admit the situation was severe enough that the President was briefed by the White House counterterrorism and Homeland Security advisor as well as Chief Of Staff Denis McDonough. Later that day, Department of Homeland Security Secretary Jeh Johnson issued a statement.

"It appears from what we know at this stage that the malfunctions at United Airlines and the (New York) stock exchange were not the result of any nefarious actor. We know less about the Wall Street Journal at this point except that their system is back up again as is the United Airlines system."

As has been their M.O. for the last several years, the administration prefers to downplay the potential threats of cyber attacks on our nation's power grid. If a cyber attack were to occur and severely damage our grid, would the government downplay that as well? Would they avoid urging American to prepare for such an event for fear of instilling panic in the streets? Is our critical infrastructure secure? Are the analysts overstating the vulnerability?

CHAPTER FIFTEEN
WHAT COULD CAUSE A CYBER WAR—
WORLD WAR C?

The speed and intensity of cyber intrusions are on the rise, increasing the chance that overuse by one or more rogue nations could escalate cyber vandalism or espionage into a devastating cyber war—*World War C.* There are several scenarios envisioned by our military and cyber analysts. Here are the most widely held theories.

Private sector cyber counter-attacks

As American corporations continue to suffer significant economic loss from accelerated intellectual property theft and disruptions to their operations from cyber attacks, private sector companies could initiate their own cyber counter-offensives. There are many options available to private sector victims of cyber intrusions. Tactics for retaliation could range from placing *honeypots* with deliberately falsified data on corporate networks (as was used in the Trans-Siberian Gas Pipeline explosion) to disrupting the networks of suspected attackers by returning the favor with their own team of cyber mercenaries.

However, this type of cyber vigilantism could quickly escalate by involving the government's protection of their private sector participants. Acting against the perpetrators of the massive cyber espionage operation might necessarily mean attacking a nation-state's military-industrial complex. Although the cyber mercenary's goal may be to target an apparently private corporation, the cyber retaliation may be dangerous because of the close relationship between quasi-public companies and their national governments in countries like

China and Russia. The country being targeted by a corporation's private retaliation for cyber intrusions may also perceive the counter offensive as a proxy attack on the security or military services of the company's home country, leading to a broader and more damaging spiral of escalation. Many wars have begun because different perceptions create different realities.

Out of control *patriotic hackers*

One of the scenarios which would result in an escalation from cyber vandalism to an all-out cyber war begins with the so-called *patriotic hackers*—a term applied to computer hackers who are strident supporters of a country and whose goal is to initiate attacks upon their beloved nation's adversaries. Because of their unpredictability and the lack of control that intelligence and military organization have over such groups, *patriotic hackers* may become over-enthusiastic, thus exceeding the policies of their governments. For example, politically motivated hackers might destroy data rather than merely conducting cyber vandalism through defacing a web site or by introducing malicious software that spreads throughout the target's network.

Many *patriotic hacker* groups are loosely affiliated with, or sanctioned by, the governments they support. But even actions by independent hackers, completely unaffiliated with a government, could set off an escalation of tensions leading to an all-out cyber war. As has been discussed, attribution for cyber exploits is hard to identify using the best of cyber forensics, and a nation-states' use of hacker proxy groups could lead some victims to see a pattern in the activity. Often, by overuse of a particular technique, a government's cyber fingerprints behind an action can be determined, despite the hacker group's lacking actual affiliation with an intelligence or military service. Assignment of attribution may get even more difficult as various proxy tools are increasingly available online which make it easier for private citizens, or for smaller and poorer states, to carry out fast, sophisticated, and untraceable cyber activity. One cyber security analyst provided two realistic examples; an attack on a

Chinese organizations' networks by hacktivists protesting the treatment of ethnic minorities, or on Russian oil companies' IT systems protesting environmental issues. Either Russia or China could view these cyber attacks as undertaken by a proxy for a Western government that could quickly lead to a spiral of retaliation.

An escalation of cyber vandalism caused by a patriotic hacker group's exploits to a perceived act of cyber warfare could occur with little or no warning. As in traditional warfare, one would hope that the most powerful nations on earth would open a dialogue, rather than react in kind, or worst.

World War C

In this final scenario, it is a very real possibility that cyber attacks can escalate into a cyber war as a tactical maneuver to supplement conventional military activity. The Russians are notorious for the use of cyber attacks to enhance its military capability, as apparently happened in the Russia-Georgia conflict, later in Estonia, and most recently in Ukraine. It is within the arsenal of the world's major military powers to use cyber weapons against strategic targets instead of more conventional strikes. As Russia has proven, a military could use cyber weapons to disrupt the network systems that modern armed forces use for communications and logistical support.

But the most deadly scenario to a nation would be the use of cyber warfare to collapse their critical infrastructure. Not only would this disrupt traditional command and control systems, but it would also effectively distract a nation's military defenses while it fills the requirement of tending to its population in need. The nature and extent of potential damage to vulnerable power grids would be hard to anticipate, and a spread of military malware beyond its intended targets—or its capture and re-use by other parties—could compound the collapse event.

The effective use of cyber warfare in this scenario would go beyond the disruption of internet or communication services. The goal of the aggressor would be to bring down the power grid, the lifeblood of any nation.

CHAPTER SIXTEEN
A MAJOR ATTACK ON AMERICA'S CRITICAL INFRASTRUCTURE

A cyber attack on America's critical infrastructure would cause chaos in the country by interrupting vital utility services for the nation.

While the stock exchange, transportation, and media are critical to the normal operations of any country, the power grid and water plants are absolute necessities to prevent mass deaths. A failure of these systems as a result of a cyber attack would cause more than serious inconveniences to the nation; the deaths would be in the millions.

There has been a rapid increase in the number of cyber attacks directed at America's power grid in recent years. They have avoided detection in many cases because of their increased complexity.

In February of 2015, the DHS Cyber Emergency Response Team issued its new ICS-CERT MONITOR report related to the period September 2014 – February 2015. According to the report, the Industrial Control Systems Cyber Emergency Response Team received and responded to nearly three hundred incidents during the government's Fiscal Year 2014, more than half of the incidents reported by asset owners and industry partners involved sophisticated cyber intrusions. The ICS/SCADA system, commonly used by major utilities, were targeted by various cyber threat actors, including criminals, rogue nations, and hacktivists.

Over fifty percent involved advanced persistent threats—APT, or sophisticated actors. In most cases, the threat actors were unknown due to a lack of attributional data. The report clearly illustrates that the nature and complexity of cyber intrusions are increasing, and the target of choice has shifted from stealing personal financial data to conducting penetration testing on major utilities.

The majority of the attacks involved entities in the energy sector followed by critical manufacturing—the manufacture of vehicles, aviation, and aerospace components. Typically, the hackers used zero-day vulnerabilities to compromise the utilities' industrial control systems, such as SCADA.

The most common flaws exploited by attackers include authentication and distributed denial of service measures. The report confirmed that the attackers used a vast range of methods for attempting to compromise utility control systems infrastructure to avoid establishing a cyber fingerprint. The tools at their disposal included malicious code, spear phishing attacks, and SQL injection attacks.

The report points out the difficulty of attribution of an incident to a particular threat actor. In the majority of cases, these offensives have gone under the radar over the years due to the high level of sophistication of the tactics and cyber-techniques.

The victims are typically unable to identify the attackers, Therefore many more incidents occur in critical infrastructure that goes unreported. Often, the forensic evidence does not point to a method used for intrusion because of a lack of detection and monitoring capabilities within the compromised network.

The DHS report concludes the U.S. power grid is highly vulnerable to cyber attacks.

The U.S. power grid is a considered a privileged target for all categories of terrorists, cyber criminals, and state-sponsored patriot hackers. Daily, they threaten the backbone of the American society. Security experts and U.S. politicians are aware that the national power grid is vulnerable to a terrorist attack.

Terrorists and rogue nations have several options to hit a power grid, from a cyber-attack on SCADA systems to an EMP attack, according to cyber security analysts. Former Secretary of Defense, William Cohen, in a 2015 interview, discussed the issue at length.

"You can do it through cyber-attacks, and that's the real threat coming up as well. We have to look at cyber-attacks being able to shut down our power grid, which you have to remember is in the private sector's hands, not the government's. And we're vulnerable," Cohen added. "It's possible and whether it's likely to happen soon remains to be seen."

"That's because the technology continues to expand, and terrorism has become democratized. Many, many people across the globe now have access to information that allows them to be able to put together a very destructive means of carrying out their terrorist plans. We're better at detecting than we were in the past. We're much more focused on integrating and sharing the information that we have, but we're still vulnerable and we'll continue to be vulnerable as long as groups can operate either on the margins or covertly to build this kind of campaigns of terror." said Cohen.

Former Department of Homeland Security Secretary Janet Napolitano echoed his sentiments. She caught everyone's attention when she said, briefly after her departure from government, that a major cyber attack on the nation's power grid *was not a matter of if, but when.*

While it is accepted in the intelligence community that state sponsored cyber-terrorists are the most likely threat actors, cyber criminals represent a serious menace as well.

Former senior CIA analyst and EMP Task Force On National

Homeland Security Director, Dr. Peter Vincent Pry, confirmed in an interview with Newsmax TV that a cyber attack against the power grid could cause serious destruction and loss of life.

The British Parliament revealed that UK Power Grid is under cyber attack from foreign hackers daily, confirming the incessant attacks on Britain's national critical infrastructure.

"Our National Grid is coming under cyber-attack not just day-by-day but minute-by-minute," said James Arbuthnot, a member of the British Parliament whose committee scrutinized the country's security policy. "There are, at the National Grid, people of very high quality who recognize the risks that these attacks pose, and who are fighting them off, but we can't expect them to fend them off forever."

The power grid is a vital system for our society, and the cyber strategy of every government must consider its protection a high priority, a terror attack would leave entire countries sitting in the dark. Several high profile cyber security firms have issued a hypothetical attack scenario and estimation of the losses—both of loss of life and economically.

What will happen in the case of a cyber-attack on a critical infrastructure in the US? What is the economic impact of a cyber-attack against America's power grid?

According to a poll of 2,173 registered voters by researchers at the Morning Consult firm, cyber attacks rank a close second to a terrorist attack on the list of biggest threats to the United States. The research showed that cyber security experts estimate the insurance industry could face losses of over twenty billion dollars.

Specifically, thirty-six percent of voters consider acts of terrorism at the top of a list of major security threats, followed by cyber attacks at thirty-two percent.

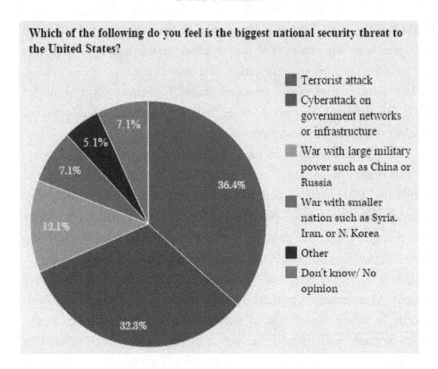

Which of the following do you feel is the biggest national security threat to the United States?

- Terrorist attack
- Cyberattack on government networks or infrastructure
- War with large military power such as China or Russia
- War with smaller nation such as Syria, Iran, or N. Korea
- Other
- Don't know/ No opinion

36.4%
32.3%
12.1%
7.1%
7.1%
5.1%

Lloyd's of London conducted a very in-depth study in 2015, *Business Blackout* that describes the impacts of a possible cyber attack on the nation's critical infrastructure. It is the first time that the insurance industry has elaborated on a similar report. According to the report prepared by Lloyd's in a joint effort with the University of Cambridge's Centre for Risk Studies, a devastating cyber attack on America's power grid would have a catastrophic impact on multiple types of insurance.

The attack scenario described by *Business Blackout* illustrates the effects of a hypothetical malware-based attack on systems that controls the U.S. power grid. In their hypothetical scenario, the attack causes an electrical blackout that plunges fifteen U.S. states and highly populated cities, including New York and Washington, into darkness. Nearly 93 million people will be affected without power in the hypothetical.

According to the researchers, the attack will cause health and safety systems to fail, disrupting water supplies as electric pumps fail. The chaos will reign causing the failure of central services, including transportation. Because the malware can infect the Internet, thereby allowing it to search and compromise fifty generators that it will destroy, there would be lengthy power outages in the region.

The total of claims paid by the insurance industry has been estimated to be included in the interval comprised between twenty and seventy billion dollars depending on the length of time necessary to remedy the scenarios designed by the researchers.

The researchers involved in the simulation have calculated the economic losses could approach $1 trillion, depending on the number of components in the power grid compromised by the attack.

Economic impacts included in the report were direct damage to assets and infrastructure, the decline in sales revenue to electricity supply companies, loss of sales revenue to business and disruption to the supply chain. In order to form their hypothesis, the experts analyzed the historical outages, estimating that currently the power interruptions, the vast majority of which last five minutes or less, already cost the US about $96 billion.The business and industrial sectors are the sectors most impacted by the attack on the power grid due to their dependency on electricity.

The Business Blackout report states evidence from historical outages, and indicative modeling suggests that power interruptions already cost the US economy roughly one hundred billion dollars a year. Under normal conditions, over ninety-five percent of outage costs are borne by the commercial and industrial sectors due to the high dependence on electricity as an input factor of production.

As explained in the report, it is important to identify the risks related to a possible cyber attack and adopt all the necessary measures to mitigate them. The protection of critical infrastructure like a power grid should be an essential part of the cyber strategy of any government.

Threat intelligence and information sharing are essential to limit the number of cyber attacks. As a result of increased awareness and recent cyber events, President Obama issued an *Executive Order Promoting Private Sector Cybersecurity Information Sharing*, confirming the administration's cyber strategy. Toward that end, in 2014 the U.S. Government issued the *Framework for Improving Critical Infrastructure Security.*

The *Framework* was published in response to Executive Order 13636, which states that "it is the Policy of the United States to enhance the security and resilience of the Nation's critical infrastructure and to maintain a cyber environment that encourages efficiency, innovation, and economic prosperity while promoting safety, security, business confidentiality, privacy, and civil liberties."

The *Framework* was designed to improve security for IT and SCADA networks deployed in sensitive industries such as energy, water, and financial services. The *Framework* stresses the information sharing on principal threats and outlines and defines the best practices that allow mitigation of the attacks. Both private and public sector organizations are encouraged to report any suspect activity for prevention and a prompt response to the incidents. The implementation of the *Framework* is in its infancy. Thus there has been little written about its success.

CHAPTER SEVENTEEN
BASED UPON WHAT WE KNOW, COULD HACKERS BRING DOWN THE U.S. POWER GRID?

It has been clearly established that various threat actors around the world have made it their goal to inflict maximum pain on the United States and one method that can be utilized is a grid down scenario, whether by electromagnetic pulse weapon, or cyber attack. The biggest fear of many political leaders and cyber security analysts, the worst case scenario, is often described in terms of a cyber attack on our critical infrastructure. These cyber war predictions almost always envision an attack on the U.S. power grid that would cause a widespread blackout.

The nation states who currently have the greatest capability to use cyber attacks to inflict broad, systemic damage on their adversaries are the well-resourced nation states who are most likely to calibrate their targeting carefully. For example, if China or the United States were to try to immobilize the entire economy of the other, they would open a serious risk of a cyber retaliation aimed at inflicting the same kind of damage, or worse. This is similar to the *mutually assured destruction* doctrine that helped restrain the use of nuclear weapons. But yet the risk remains because, in the cyber realm, the bad actors may have nothing to lose. Think North Korea.

In 2014 testimony before the House Intelligence Committee, NSA Director Admiral Michael Rogers went into some detail on those risks:

Admiral Rogers was questioned about one such hypothetical. "If it was determined that malware was on those critical infrastructure systems, can you be a little more definitive about what does that mean? If I'm on that system, and I want to do some harm, what does that do? Do the lights go out? Do we stop pumping water? What does that mean? And the fact that it was there does that mean they already have the capability to 'flip the switch' if they wanted to?"

Admiral Rogers responded: "Well let me address the last part first. There shouldn't be any doubt in our minds that there are nation-states and groups out there that have the capability to do that. To enter our systems, to enter those industrial control systems, and to shut down, forestall our ability to operate, our basic infrastructure. Whether it's generating power across this nation, or whether it's moving water and fuel, once you're into the system and you're able to do manipulate that. It enables you to do things like, if I want to tell power turbines to go offline and stop generating power, you can do that. If I wanted to segment the transmission system so that you couldn't distribute the power that was coming out of the power stations, this would enable you to do that. It allows you to shut down very segmented, very tailored parts of our infrastructure."

A number of media outlets and cyber security professionals interpreted these comments as a claim by the NSA that a country like China could take down our nation's power grid. Is a widespread, national blackout caused by hackers a realistic possibility? The power grid is vulnerable to attack. Adm. Rogers' testimony was extremely important as it provided a strong, authoritative voice to what is an urgent problem facing this country right now—**America's critical infrastructure is vulnerable to attack, it's a complicated problem to fix, and an attack is imminent.**

PART SEVEN
PREPARING FOR CYBER WARFARE

Because you never know when the day before...

is the day before. Prepare for tomorrow

@FreedomPreppers

CHAPTER EIGHTEEN
CYBER WAR IMPLICATIONS
FOR BUSINESS

Cybergeddon or World War C is not here yet, but it might be tomorrow. You never know when the day before—is the day before.

Under the most likely scenarios, the effects of a cyber war on most businesses are more likely to be disruptive than apocalyptic for two main reasons. Cyber intrusions can immobilize your business operations for hours and maybe days. Modern critical infrastructures tend to have enough built-in stop-gap measures and protections to prevent a cataclysmic crash of the entire power grid simultaneously or for an extended period.

The business of cyber terrorism is growing in many directions. There is a growing gray market for cyber weapons able to exact more powerful exploits—directed against utility and industrial control systems. These hacking tools are becoming more readily available to governments of smaller nations and even non-state groups, like ISIS, that would have less to lose in a cyber exchange than a major power. In addition, the number of potential targets of hacker activity is growing exponentially as technological advances allow interconnectivity of networks subject to being targeted.

The accelerating globalization of many business entities will also leave them increasingly vulnerable to disruption from cyber war even if it does not involve their home government. The public sector relies on R&D and manufacturing that are often based in third-world countries. These important sources of innovation and revenue could be cut off, at least temporarily, by the deployment of cyber weapons. Cyber war operations could also disrupt supply chains and support services. Tensions between China and other nations in Southeast Asia could disrupt call center operations in India or the manufacture of specialty parts for global supply chains in the Philippines.

A cyber war could disrupt business operations across much of the United States economy. Industries closely tied to military capabilities would quickly become the front lines of such a conflict. The defense industry, airlines, energy companies, pharmaceutical manufacturers and healthcare providers, commercial Internet service providers and telecommunications firms are just a few of the industries that serve military and other government operations. Then there are the utilities that supply power and water to government facilities.

Business, nonprofit, and government leaders should anticipate significant indirect effects. Companies around the world could experience damage from malware or a massive DDoS attack that a hacker introduced into their business networks via customers, suppliers, perhaps even employees' personal contacts and electronic devices that had been connected to other corporate networks. As the world becomes more interconnected, the threat of cyber intrusion grows.

A cyber war—like any war—is an outcome no one wants. But, given the ready availability and growing power of cyber weapons, the plethora of potential military targets on IT networks, and the many points of friction between competing nation states, this is an outcome we could all soon face with little or no warning. Organizations of all kinds need to be able to protect their most valuable assets when a cyber war comes or their business will risk becoming collateral damage.

There should be no doubt as to who handles an organization's response to a possible cyberwar or other security challenges. Although cybersecurity programs are typically executed by a Chief Information Officer, the entire leadership team must be committed to cyber preparedness. Beyond enhancing resiliency, this type of preparation will build a mindset that is better able to recognize current and future security risks, navigate the threat landscape in pursuit of business opportunities, and allocate security resources more efficiently.

Planning for a cyber war should include knowing how a potential adversary looks at an organization. The identity of enemies, the type of intrusion they might undertake, and the hacker tools they might use are all factors to consider. A thorough internal assessment will determine how an organization conducts business with an eye towards potential cyber vulnerabilities.

Another key element is understanding whether an organization has a secure internal business network. Many times, corporate assets—and corresponding vulnerabilities—are part of a global network. Supply chains, service providers and strategic partners, employees, and customers are all dependent upon one another and an attack on any one of these interconnected entities could negatively impact the entire business.

Every private sector business, regardless of size, should remain informed, aware, and secure. Most organizations will be best prepared for the contingency of cyber war by focusing on the following:

Protect those assets that are most valuable to the organization, and desirable by the cyber intruders;

Implement a cyber security plan that will not only protect a business in the event of cyber war but put it ahead of the pack in the global marketplace afterward; and

Study the activities of policymakers and cyber security experts to keep up-to-date on threats.

CHAPTER NINETEEN
IT'S TIME TO GET READY FOR THE
COMING CYBER WAR

First, let's summarize the scope of the problem. We've known for years that America's infrastructure isn't as robust as it should be.

During the Northeast blackout of 2003, for example, a large portion of the Northeastern and Midwestern United States, together with some of Canada was blacked out as a result of a minor software bug at a FirstEnergy electrical station in Ohio. This event, combined with out-of-date hardware across the nation's power grid and lax security, could easily result in an opportunity for hackers to take down critical infrastructure across the country.

The FBI recently caught three Russian operatives attempting to trigger a *Flash Crash* in the United States stock market like the one that occurred in 2010. During that event, massive computer networks—trading at millisecond speeds—over-corrected and dropped the Dow Jones Industrial Average 1,000 points in just minutes.

Hackers don't have to attack Wall Street directly. One cyber attack, like the one that recently involved incorrect information posted on Twitter, can cause major panic in the financial markets. In 2013, the Syrian Electronic Army hacked the Associated Press Twitter account and tweeted that there had been an explosion at the White House and President Obama was injured. This caused panic trading that created a temporary loss of around $136.5 billion in the S&P.

In 2014, Ransomware hackers knocked an unidentified radio station in Louisiana off the air. The radio station, which had a firewall in place, was running an older version of Windows XP on its computers. In this case, the hacker's goal was extortion or ransom. But in the event of a terrorist activity, this could be a method to disrupt critical communications networks. Despite the hacker's goal, it's still evidence that hackers are capable of just about anything.

If cyber terrorists didn't attack electronically, they might cut Internet cables manually. This happened in San Francisco recently which resulted in an Internet outage after vandals broke into a secure vault and cut an important Internet backbone cable.

In 2015, the Department of Defense accidentally released an 800-page document on the Aurora Project. It was a detailed analysis of how hackers could take down the U.S. power grid and water systems. It wasn't very comforting as it detailed potentially catastrophic loss of life.

Recent cyber attacks reveal it isn't only the power grid that is vulnerable. The U.S. air traffic control system is getting a major upgrade, and it brings with it some problems that a hacker can exploit. This may have been the reason for the attack upon the United Airlines' computer system which grounded 4,900 flights and delayed travel across the country.

At the same time, another *computer glitch* shut down the New York Stock Exchange for four hours and brought trading to a standstill. Clearly, hackers are busy trying to cause other problems.

This book has been replete with the various ways hackers could launch a cyber attack that causes major disruption. However, there are two more unexpected cyber tools available to hackers that you might not have considered.

Our enemies test our defenses every second of every day. As has been stated repeatedly in this book by experts across the spectrum; *it's not a matter of if a cyber attack will be successful in collapsing our power grid; it's a matter of when.*

CHAPTER TWENTY
WE ARE ALL PREPPERS NOW

The threats we face are many. At FreedomPreppers.com, Americans are urged to prepare for a worst-case scenario. If nothing happens, you've lost nothing. For the United States, short of nuclear annihilation, the worst case scenario is an extended grid down scenario.

The way you protect yourself isn't very high-tech. In fact, you're going to be better off going low-tech.

Where do you begin in formulating a Preparedness Plan? An entire preparedness guide, hundreds of pages long, may still not adequately cover the elements of a comprehensive preparedness plan. The numerous disaster preparedness guides, blogs, and professional videos are all excellent resources. But where does one start?

Essentially, it all boils down to:

Beans, Band-Aids & Bullets

Well, of course there is much more to developing a preparedness plan than the *big three*, but all preparedness experts know these are the basics. Many preppers are well organized and rely heavily upon checklists. We urge you to review Appendix B which provides a summary as well as a link to a free pdf download of an extensive preparedness checklist. Preppers constantly update their checklists to insure they didn't overlook anything. You will as well.

As you review the following, keep in mind certain basic principles when preparing your plan.

The survival rule of threes: You can only live three minutes without air; three hours without shelter in extreme conditions; three days without water; and three weeks without food. This helps you prioritize your preps for a post collapse survival situation.

The prepper rule of redundancy: Three is two, two is one, and one is none. When your prepper supplies run out, you can't drive down to Wal-Mart and restock.

Building your prepper supplies to an acceptable level for long term survival requires baby steps. Thus, survival planning starts with the perfect trinity of prepping—*beans, band-aids and bullets.* Clearly, an oversimplification of what a preparedness plan entails, but it is a pretty good reflection of what you better have covered. This is a well known expression within the prepper community as it outlines the essentials that you will need in the event of TEOTWAWKI—the end of the world as we know it.

In summary, *beans* will include your prepper supplies, the items in your prepper pantry and water. *Band-aids* will refer to all things medical. *Bullets* represent the weapons and ammunition necessary to protect yourself, your family and your preps.

Beans – Your Prepper Pantry

What is in your prepper pantry? Right now, honest assessment. How many days could your family survive on what's in your house right now? Most American households have less than seven days of food on hand.

Building a prepper pantry is one of those lifelines that take both time and planning to make it fully functional. Ideally, you want to store shelf stable foods that your family normally consumes, as well as find foods that serve multiple purposes. Stocking your prepper pantry should involve a combination of ready to eat food and beverages to last your family many months plus long term food storage for a year or more.

Overall, your prepper pantry should reflect an abundance of the foods that you eat on a regular basis. Utilize a first in, first out rotation. This is a mistake many new preppers make. They buy food they don't eat on a regular basis. Store foods that have a long shelf life, that don't require refrigeration after opening, and that are easy to cook off the grid.

Our suggested preparedness plan includes non-perishable foods on our shelves to last us one year. Then we have canned vegetables, fruit, and meats created throughout the year. Finally, dried goods such as beans, rice, pasta, and oatmeal are stored utilizing Mylar Bags and desiccant packs (this technique is discussed in depth on the Freedom Preppers website) which can last for up to twenty years.

The following foods are all popular food staples that should be considered as "must haves" for your Prepper Pantry. The advantages to storing these items are they encompass all of the key consideration points listed above. Best of all, these items are very affordable and versatile, thus making them worthy of being on your storage shelves for extended emergencies. You'll find most of these items in your pantry already. Try to increase the quantity each week and place them into rotation. Use this list as a starting point on beginning or extending your Prepper Pantry. Always keep your family's food preferences and dietary needs in mind when investing in your food supply. This list is very basic, but a good start. The checklist in Appendix B is helpful as well.

- Dried legumes such as beans, lentils, and peas

- Rice, lots of rice

- Pasta and sauces

- Oatmeal, Cream of Wheat, and cereals

- Canned meat, fish, soups, fruits, and vegetables

- Peanut Butter

- Packaged Meals (macaroni and cheese, hamburger helper, Ramen noodles

- Seasonings and cooking oils

- Flour, salt, sugar, corn meal, and powdered cheeses

- Powdered drinks like milk, Tang and Gatorade; Tea Bags

Here are some additional considerations.

Food - If you would like to start storing food there are some things to think about. How long will the food last? Is this something that you and your family will realistically eat? Will the food survive if there is a disaster and no electricity? How will you cook the food you have stored? The amount of food stored ultimately depends on the person that is storing it. But, keep in mind that you need to have enough food for the amount of time a foreseen disaster will last. If you are just preparing for a short term disaster then maybe only a few days to a week of food is necessary. If your preparations need to last after a massive break down of society or a major disaster, you may want to have a few months to multiple years of food stockpiled. Also you may want to raise your own livestock and have a fruit and vegetable garden. Hunting and Fishing are also a great way to get food. Just a note, all grocery stores combined in one city usually only have about 3 days' worth of food for the entire city. This is known as *just-in-time inventory*, and will be gone within hours when a collapse event becomes apparent.

Heirloom Seeds – While technically not food, yet, the ability to grow your own food will be critical to sustain yourself after your food supplies run out. Besides, before the SHTF, *growing your own food is like printing your own money*. And, it's good practice.

Water – FEMA claims that each adult needs one gallon of water per person per day. This is wholly inadequate. While this quantity may keep you hydrated, it will not be sufficient to maintain your location. When there is no water coming out of the sink where will you find fresh, clean water? You may want to keep water stockpiled as well. There are a couple options for this.

The basic principles revolve around *water catchment, purification, and storage*. Again, water management is a subject for an entire book. But consider this. In third world countries, dysentery is one of the major causes of death. In a grid down scenario caused by a cyber attack, or otherwise, America will be set back into the nineteenth century from a technology standpoint. Drinking unclean water can kill you.

There are options. You can keep water bottles or gallon containers full. There are also water tanks that come in various sizes anywhere from under a hundred gallons up to thousands of gallons. If you are lucky enough to be near a river or lake, this may be a good source of water. There are many types and sizes of water filters that don't need electricity and make even the worst water safe to drink. There are also tablets that can be placed in water to purify it. A well would also be a fantastic water source, but can be quite pricey to build. Ultimately, there are many options, but it is a good idea to know about the natural water sources in your area.

Pets - Finally, please do not forget your pets. They are family too and dogs, in particular, may be a useful asset in your home's defenses.

Bandaids – Your Armageddon Medicine Cabinet

After a collapse event, you will probably not have ready access to a dentist or doctor, much less a hospital. Available treatment will be scarce and required medicines even scarcer. When you become injured or sick, help will not be on the way. You will become the primary care physician for your prepper group.

Survival Medicine requires you to have a substantial preppers First Aid Kit, complete with over-the-counter and pharmacy medications. You will need to gain the knowledge necessary to diagnose and treat a variety of illnesses and injuries, including dental care.

Preventative Medicine - Though not a conventional aspect of beans, bullets, and band-aids, staying in shape and being healthy is one of the best ways to prevent problems after any collapse event. When we are healthy we are able to work harder and more efficiently. Being healthy and in shape can also promote productivity. Some of the ways to prepare for an end of the world scenario are to eat right, exercise regularly, and keep an active lifestyle. Knowledge of minor medical procedures is also a great way to prepare.

Prescription Medications - If you need a certain prescription to maintain a productive lifestyle, make sure to have a surplus of them on hand. There are some doctors that will give extra prescriptions for the purpose of preparing and stockpiling, so the beans, bullets and bandaids theory suggests asking and explaining your situation to your physician. Additionally, there are some medicines that should be kept on hand; antibiotics are an important one. We suggest stockpiling fish antibiotics as they are some of the most useful to treat infections. But don't forget the many over the counter medicines that are used regularly. These can include aspirin, allergy medicines, cold or flu remedies, diarrhea medicines, stool softeners among many more. Medical supplies such as those found in a first aid or trauma kit are very important. For instance, how will you dress a wound or set a broken bone? It is good to have bandaids, bandages, braces, splints, and thermometers on hand. The more you know and have increases the chances of surviving.

Hygiene - Maintaining personal hygiene and sanitation after the collapse event is critical. Ingesting bacteria may kill you without access to proper medical care. Consider this: How many rolls of toilet paper do your family use a day? What will you use as an alternative when you run out? Where do you plan to poop when the SHTF? Got the picture?

Prepping for hygiene may be as simple as obtaining multiples of everyday household items. Savvy preppers know they need to stockpile a supply of food and water but hygiene products are essential to decrease the spread of disease and illness. It's also helps you maintain a sense of normalcy.

In a post-SHTF world, sanitation and hygiene will be important to keep yourself and your family healthy. Running water may no longer be an option or a healthy choice, and you need to know how to practice good hygiene, proper sanitation and keep your environment healthy. These are all very important considerations in a SHTF situation. Due to a lack of available medical facilities or treatment, health and disease prevention are going to be more important and more difficult to treat than ever after the TEOTWAWKI.

Sanitation items are easy to gather. You may prefer a pre-assembled emergency kit which already contains necessary items for grooming and sanitation. Because many kit items are sold as a unit, you may find that purchasing a kit is an inexpensive and convenient way to prepare all that you'll need during an emergency. Another option may be to assemble your own emergency kit so you can choose brands or items your family is accustomed to using. Often, you can purchase your favorite brand of soap, toothpaste, shampoo, toilet paper, deodorant and other items in bulk or extra saving packages so you can afford to set some aside for your emergency kit.

Here are some items to consider:

Toilet Paper - When it comes to emergencies, any kind of toilet paper is a luxury. By preparing ahead of time, you can ensure that you don't experience unneeded discomfort by having to get used to a new texture of paper. Also keep in mind that it is common for those in emergency situations to develop stress and diet related stomach problems that can intensify your sanitation difficulties.

Toothbrush + Oral Hygiene - People with sensitive teeth may want to store their preferred brand of toothbrush in their emergency kit. It is probably a wise idea to store several toothbrushes to give away to someone who neglected to store one. It may also have another useful purpose such as cleaning or scrubbing.

Toothpaste, Mouthwash, and Breath Fresheners - Emergencies present stressful situations where human communication is crucial. Sometimes water is scarce or unavailable which causes dryness in your mouth. A breath freshener may be a nice addition to your preparedness supplies.

Feminine Hygiene Products - It is important to be prepared in all areas. These items are definitely important to have available in any emergency situation.

Deodorant - With several choices of deodorants including anti-perspirants, made-for-a-woman brands, gelled, etc., you may want to decide ahead of time what you'll need during an emergency.

Air fresheners or deodorants may also increase your level of comfort during an emergency.

Hair Supplies Shampoo, conditioner, hairspray, combs, brushes, and other items may not be necessary for survival, but they can help make an emergency situation more comfortable and clean. Be sure to store smaller sanitation items in your emergency kit and be aware that you can overstuff your emergency kit. If it is too heavy, you may not be able to leave with it during an emergency.

Medications for diarrhea, constipation, headaches, allergy and other minor conditions should also be included in kits for added comfort.

Laundry Detergent and Soap - During some emergencies, you may be required to evacuate the area or may be stranded in some remote area. Because you won't have lots of clothing, you will want detergent to clean your clothes and soap for bathing and for washing utensils.

Hand sanitizers are essential to keep in your bug out bag as well.

Bathing - You can prevent illness by washing your hands often; before eating, after using the bathroom, after you change a diaper, and any other time you may need to freshen up. Because water is such a precious commodity during an emergency, you should remember to use purified drinking water first for drinking, cooking, washing dishes and then for other purposes. Be organized and choose a designated bathing area. If you wash in a river or stream use biodegradable soap and always be aware of others who may be down stream. With a little soap you can also wash yourself in the rain. Other washing alternatives include moist towelettes, a spray bottle, sanitizing lotions, or a wet washcloth. Be sure to wear shoes to prevent parasitic infections and to protect you from cuts and puncture wounds that can easily become infected.

Sanitation Area - Choosing the right location for your sanitation needs is as important as staying clean. Your waste place must be located downhill from any usable water source. It should also be a few hundred feet from any river, stream, or lake. It also helps to have your waste place downwind from your living area, and yet not too far from your camp that the distance discourages people from using it.

Luggable Loo - With a little preparation, you can have a decent emergency toilet. If you have a five gallon plastic bucket lined with a heavy-duty garbage bag, you have a toilet. Don't forget to add deodorized cat litter to assist with the odor. Make sure you have a lid to cover it. A plastic toilet seat can be purchased to fit on the bucket for a more comfortable seat. If you don't have an extra plastic bucket available, you can make a latrine by digging a long trench approximately one foot wide and 12 to 18 inches deep and cover as you go. When you dig too deep a latrine it can slow the bacterial breakdown process. The long latrine approach is appropriate for large groups camping in one spot for a long period.

Getting Rid of Refuse - If you cannot dispose of refuse properly you should always bury biodegradable garbage and human waste to avoid the spread of disease by rats and insects. Dig a pit 12 to 18 inches deep and at least 50 feet but preferably 200 plus feet downhill and away from any well, spring, or water supply. Fill the pit with the refuse and cover with dirt. For back-country hikers, packing out all solid waste is always appropriate, and some authorities at high-use rivers usually require this process. You can make a seat for your latrine by laying logs across the hole, leaving an area open for you to use. After use, cover the waste with small amounts of dirt to decrease the odor. A covered toilet reduces more of the odor than an open one. Make a toilet cover with wood or a large leaf. If the odor becomes unbearable, fill in the latrine completely with dirt and dig a new one. Build a new seat and burn the old wood that you used for the last toilet.

Keeping Food Sanitary - All food scraps should be either burned or buried in a pit far from your living area to keep bears and other wild animals away from you. Keep all your food covered and off the ground. You may keep your food in a tree, but be sure tree dwelling creatures can't get into it. Replace all lids on water bottles and other containers immediately after use. Do not wash your dishes in the area where you get your drinking water supply. Instead, wash your dishes away from a stream. Use clean plates or eat out of the original food containers to prevent the spread of germs. Wash and peel all fruits and vegetables before eating. Prepare only as much as will be eaten at each meal.

Bullets – Your SHTF Defense Tools

Bottom Line: If you can't defend it, it isn't yours.

Conceptually, preparation without security is meaningless. It doesn't matter if you hate guns. Perhaps your political or religious beliefs prevent you from committing acts of violence, or self-defense. After TEOTWAWKI, the world will become a brutal place. The world we live in will not be unicorns and rainbows. Unless you are prepared to give up your preps, or even your life, all preppers need a security plan.

Actual security countermeasures can be quite complex, but they generally conform to the five principles of prepper security. A security plan involves the five D's:

Deter ~ Deny ~ Detect ~ Delay ~ Defend

The first *D* is *deter*. The first goal is to deter an attack by giving the appearance of a robust security program and substantial physical barriers. Deterrence also comes from aggressive defensive positioning. Countermeasures include an alert security force, vehicle checkpoints & searches, guard towers, visible weapons positions, lighting and armed patrols pushing out from the immediate perimeter.

The second principle is to *deny* access through physical barriers and security forces. The types of physical barriers include trenches, fences, concertina wire, razor ribbon, Hesco baskets and concrete barriers. In the absence of construction resources, security guard forces can be positioned to deny access. However, the fewer the physical barriers in place, the greater the security forces required to deny access into your perimeter.

The third *D* is *detect*. Early detection of an attempted intrusion or breach of your perimeter is critical to an effective defensive response. Detection is best achieved through open ground, cleared area and alert security personnel. Assuming a *grid down* scenario, this can be augmented with guard dogs, trip flares, battery operated alarm systems and other noise or light generating devices.

The fourth principle is to *delay* your aggressor. When your physical barriers or security forces cannot stop an attack, they should at least be positioned to delay the approach. Additional barriers allow your security forces the time to regroup, reassess and reengage the approaching attack. An effective delaying tactic will allow for reinforcements of your perimeter security forces.

The fifth *D* is *defend,* or as some might say—*destroy.* To put it bluntly, *kill or be killed.* Without rule of law—WROL—the Rules of Engagement with your adversaries will change. Make no mistake, *defend,* or the concept of *self-defense,* will be defined differently after a collapse event. The best defense is to destroy your enemy with whatever weapons are available to you. Otherwise, the sixth *D* results—*deceased.*

But, if you follow proper OPSEC, Operational Security, discussed at length below, you can minimize the number of threats that you face—especially if you follow disciplined OPSEC prior to the collapse event. Otherwise, you will face the sixth *D*.

Protection - Having a way to protect you and your family is very important during trying times as people in desperate situations will take desperate measures. Guns are a very important part of protection and may be able to diffuse a situation where talking and negotiating do not solve the situation. There are many different types of guns and many theories on which ones to own. Of course, any gun is better than no gun, but remember, each type of gun has different uses in a variety of situations. If your target is relatively close, a shotgun or pistol may be the best option. If your target is 60 yards or more away, a rifle is probably the best option. However, protection is not just limited to guns. Reusable and quiet weapons such as bows or knives are great to have because you constantly run the risk of depleting your bullet stockpile. Protection could also be in the form of a fence or barbed wire outside your home that deters thieves and other mischievous people.

Hunting- This also goes into the food category of beans, bullets and band-aids. In order to hunt efficiently and effectively, you need to know which hunting weapons to purchase and use. A .22 rifle would be much better for squirrel and varmint hunting than an AR-15. However, a .308 caliber rifle would be more effective for hunting deer or other big game animals. A bow may be better in any situation, as it is silent and will not arouse attention like a gun. Another great idea is the use of traps. These are reusable and are semi-passive ways of finding food. They can also protect your home from intruders. In the forest and plains areas, squirrels, elk, deer, birds, turkeys and water fowl are all great sources of protein.

Finally, a word about *operational security—OPSEC*. This brings us to another important axiom of prepping:

Tell No One About Your Preps!
The prepper's creed begins:
If you don't talk, no one will hear and if no one else hears, no one else will know.

Operational Security, or OPSEC, for Preppers is a discipline, a mindset. It is simply denying an adversary, present or future, vital information that could harm you or benefit them.

Prior to collapse, OPSEC involves curtailing your activities on social media or not bragging about your weapons cache.

As kids we found comfort in our homes with our families, maybe hiding under the covers or with a fave blankie. As we grow up, our concerns may focus on job security, financial security and general home security. Now we are big boys and girls—preparing for TEOTWAWKI. Security takes on a whole new meaning when you have to fear armed marauders streaming down your driveway to take your preps, or worst. Your favorite blankie won't help you.

Once there is a life changing collapse event you may take comfort in knowing you're well prepped with all the beans, band-aids, and bullets a well prepared family could need. Well, guess what? Your failure to abide by OPSEC guidelines will quickly make you a target. There are relatively simple SOP—standard operating procedures—for survival groups who've advanced their level of preparation. How can you avoid armed confrontations with the marauders? What should you do prior to the collapse event in order to keep your preps hidden from the world?

Pre-Collapse: Getting Others to Prep

Getting other people to prep is far easier said than done. If it were easy to convince people to spend their hard earned money on a possible bad future, then we'd all be prepared and there wouldn't be a fear of looting and raiding. But it isn't easy and those threats are real.

When first talking to someone about prepping, you need to understand your audience. This means that if you're talking to a hard-core outdoorsman you can bring up far more *survival-esque* components to prepping while a friend that is just talking about a natural disaster should be eased into it more.

Secondly, it's important to focus on the need to prep over the possible reasons. People don't like thinking about economic collapse or cyber warfare, so instead of hearing you talk about prepping, those people will instead argue the finer points of why those things can't happen. If you focus on the possibility of something making food, water, or essentials like toilet paper hard to get, it only makes sense to prepare for that possibility. Whatever the case, getting people on board by scaring them doesn't work, but getting them to understand their lives without the essentials is a sure fire way to get them signed up.

Once you get friends and family on board with prepping for them, it's easier to talk with them and for everyone to help each other. There's something to be said for acting alone—*the lone wolf prepper*, but a little help will never hurt. If you make the determination to form a group, you can proceed with caution.

Pre-Collapse: Forming a prepper group

As preppers, you face a conundrum. Should you be part of a prepper group or should you be a lone wolf prepper? There are benefits and detriments to both options. Here are some considerations in forming a prepper group.

One of the first things a new prepper typically wants to do is reach out to other like-minded people in their area about prepping and trying to form a prepper group. Unless there is an established and open group in the area, it's often very difficult to form a post-collapse team. Preppers are naturally cautious about discussing prepping with people they don't already know. Unless the group is actively looking for new members, you might not even know about a group in your area.

If you are serious about preparing then you have probably come to the realization that you will not be able to do everything yourself when SHTF. Just the day-to-day chores of collecting firewood, sanitation issues, cooking, food procurement, and cleaning without modern technology, will be overwhelming for a family but when you have the added issue of providing your own security you quickly realize you will need help in maintaining security.

A prepper group is an association of people that have agreed to help each other out after a collapse event. The level of help depends on the scenario, the people involved, and the community. Some prepper groups encompass an entire small town or community. Typically, the residents intend to stay in their own homes but agree to provide mutual security and aid on a community-wide scale. Because of their size, these types of groups are rare, and formed post-collapse.

The most common type of group is a loosely organized group of people that may or may not live close to each other but have general plans to provide mutual aid. They might meet together on a regular basis to discuss different scenarios, take classes together, and combine orders for bulk purchasing. Some are well organized while others just pay lip service to the concept. A prepper group like this might be beneficial during the planning stage, but in an actual event the distance between them will make mutual aid impossible.

The next prepper group is a collaboration of several like-minded individuals that have made a plan, practiced their plan, and have a mutually agreed upon location to execute that plan as a group. They live fairly close to each other but instead of trying to stay in their various locations recognize the importance of being together to provide strength in numbers. This is the best case scenario.

Putting together a prepper group does not mean you find a group of survivalists and band together, there are several things you need to

consider when deciding if someone is right for your group. Factors include:
1. What are they prepping for?
2. What skills or supplies do they bring to the table?
3. How many in their group and their relationship to each other
4. How committed are they?

When we look at forming our prepping group we have to consider if the people are like-minded, their skills, commitment, and who they bring with them. Later, for recruiting purposes, we also need to consider how many people we will need to accomplish what needs to be done

Recently, a Prepper in the Tampa, Florida area learned a hard lesson in choosing members for his preppers group. Many of the newest members had prior felonies which prohibited them from owning or possessing firearms. Further, this Florida prepper engaged in questionable conduct such as building pipe bombs and making veiled threats against law enforcement. When one of his new members of the group was arrested on unrelated charges, they turned snitch and wore a wire during the prepper's group meetings. The end result—the leader of the group is going to prison while the snitch walks free.

The debate will always rage as to whether you should be a member of a preppers group or a lone wolf prepper. Regardless of how you define your preppers group, there are common issues when determining who to let into *The Club*. It is a private membership which should always practice OPSEC due to the sensitive information everyone in the group has access to. You need to give careful consideration to the people becoming part of your group. In general, this is not an easy topic, as there are no fast and simple rules. The average human being is a complex bag of emotions and logic, to which fields of science have been dedicated to understanding. Therefore, it is not surprising when the person you thought to be a stable individual turns out to be not much more than a basket case.

Consider this. Choosing members of a preppers group is a lot like courting; you cannot really tell if they are right for you from just a few dates. Sure, we've all heard of love at first sight. However, given time, a person's true colors shine through. Being part of a group is not much different. There will be differences, arguments, heated debates, betrayals, and various other emotional conflicts. All of which need to be addressed, particularly since this group is supposed to be like a second family to you.

One very important aspect to keep in mind is what happens when someone stops being a group member. Though it may seem like many people would make a good group member, most will turn out to be incompatible with you and your group. Some people are very good at hiding who they really are, even after knowing someone for years. What has the newly ejected member learned about you, your family, and your preparedness plan? They may get kicked out of the group or they may decide to leave voluntarily. Either way, this person becomes a security risk.

When looking at group preparedness, remember that a long-term crisis scenario will require large amounts of labor for survival. Therefore, unless you are creating a specific paramilitary team, no one should be automatically discounted because of any disabilities or shortcomings (such as having a lack of gear). Look at each prospective member on a case-by-case basis, weighing their strengths and weaknesses, while keeping in mind that everyone has something to contribute. Finding group members is a tedious process, but the gains accomplished by having a group of people you can depend on are immeasurable.

Your survival may depend on it.

Post-collapse: How to Assimilate with your neighbors to form a group

These are all considerations of OPSEC for preppers that can be implemented prior to the collapse event. After TEOTWAWKI, when other factors like a grid down scenario come into play, OPSEC becomes less technology oriented.

After collapse, OPSEC will require you to resist the urge to step up and be the new leader of any newly formed survival group. One of the biggest mistakes preppers can make is to tell the wrong person or people about it. While helping people in a time of need is one of the most selfless things you can do, if you're the only person prepared in your neighborhood and everyone comes looking to you for help, all your pre-collapse OPSEC will be wasted as desperate people attempt to take the things you've worked so hard to save. We believe that it is better to be safe, keep our preparedness plans to ourselves, than to be sorry.

While you don't want to tell the world about your plans, it's expected that you want to share with close friends, family and possibly trusted coworkers. To help you understand who you should tell and who you shouldn't, we've put together a few points.

Complete privacy is nearly impossible to keep, especially when you will surely need help with something at some point. It will be very difficult to survive on your own. The biggest reason to form a survival group in our opinion is to maintain security. After collapse, your world will become much smaller. Your neighborhood will become your universe. Focus on establishing a group of neighbors first, and then look outward for like-minded thinkers.

The goal is to survive and if possible looters know what you have, that survival will be a big challenge. Within days if not hours of the collapse event, your neighbors will begin to gather to seek information. You will have a decision to make. Step up and be the leader of the group, or lay back and observe. We are in favor of continuing your OPSEC practice after collapse, and avoid a leadership role at first.

Here are the steps we recommend you take after a collapse event:

1. Take a day to gather information and assess the extent of the collapse. Observe your neighbors to gauge their reaction.

2. Maintain a heightened state of awareness. Every action and reaction of your neighbors should be observed, and not dismissed.

3. Be polite to everyone you deal with, but do so with confidence. You do not want to be perceived as weak.

4. Learn about the people around you from reliable sources. Immediately attempt to identify troublemakers.

5. Identify cliques within your neighborhood, and identify individuals or families to approach. You have to establish trust.

6. Initially, don't worry about ascertaining the level of other people's preps. Avoid suspicion by not being to inquisitive.

7. If a neighborhood meeting is called, determine who the organizers are. Typically, these individuals will be type A, overbearing temperaments.

8. Don't make waves. Better to remain quiet, than to argue. Your job is not to take control, or provide information.

9. Conceal your weapons, and do not discuss your preps, ever.

In summary, focus on your immediate family. You shouldn't tell anyone else your plan. This means if you tell your parents that live outside your house (which of course you will) you need to save supplies for them as well. If you tell your close friends, you need food and water for them, too. If you tell anyone they immediately become part of your plan. This is why the final step is getting those special people in your life to prep as well. This way, you now have a network of trusted preppers that can help one another now and when times get tough. Once you have them all at your location, then you can begin to take a more active role in your neighborhood survival group. Your close-knit group of family and friends can defend your preps in case there is an uprising amongst your neighbors.

So the big question is *who should I tell about my prepping?* The answer is anyone you feel comfortable surviving TEOTWAWKI with. If you want to house enough supplies for all your neighbors to come enjoy, tell them at your own risk. Even then you run the risk of them telling their friends and so on until you have 100 people at your door looking for a handout. Help people with knowledge and never let on to the size of your prep or the weapons you have. Getting to know your neighbors will be a big help. You will be able to determine who has the will and aptitude to survive a collapse event. After collapse, cautiously approach those neighbors to form alliances and encourage them to use their skills to help them and your group.

This is only a start to the concept of beans, bullets and band-aids. The one thing I haven't discussed yet is the importance of research and knowledge. If money is an issue, this is a great place to start. This necessary step to survival just happens to be free. There are many great books and tutorials online that will teach you anything from CPR and fishing to gardening at no cost. Now that you know about beans, bullets and bandaids, you can start preparing for any scenario you see fit.

John F. Kennedy once said *the time to repair the roof is when the sun is shining*. Because you never know when the day before—is the day before. Prepare for tomorrow.

Thanks for reading!

SIGN UP to Bobby Akart's mailing list to receive a FREE book in one of my other bestselling series. You'll also be one of the first to receive news about new releases in The Boston Brahmin Series and the Prepping for Tomorrow series.

Visit Bobby Akart's website for informative blog entries on preparedness, writing and his latest contribution to the American Preppers Network.

www.BobbyAkart.com

Stop by the Boston Brahmin website to dig deeper into the history, characters and real-life events that inspired the series.

www.TheBostonBrahmin.com

Visit the Freedom Preppers website to learn about all aspects of preparedness and the threats we face.

www.FreedomPreppers.com

APPENDIX A

The following is an excerpt from Amazon Best-Selling Author
Bobby Akart
CYBER ATTACK - Available on Amazon
http://goo.gl/cRBW8O

CHAPTER 1

May 8, 2016
3:07 p.m.
American Airlines Flight 129
33,000 Feet
Near St. Louis, Missouri

"Good afternoon from the flight deck. This is Captain Randy Gray, and it is my honor to pilot our American Airlines Boeing 757 into Washington Dulles this afternoon. We have reached our cruising altitude of thirty-three thousand feet, after averting the initial turbulence caused by the area of weather north of the Dallas–Fort Worth metro area. With a little help from a tailwind, we should arrive on time at Washington Dulles International by two o'clock local time," said Gray. "I will be turning off the Fasten Seat Belt signs to allow you free access to our newly enhanced cabin. Our flight attendants will begin cabin service shortly. As always, we thank you for flying American Airlines."

Gray began his career as a pilot in 1989 with Command Airways, a small regional carrier based in upstate New York. Initially checked out on the ATR 42, a Czech-made plane, Gray continued his training and became a highly respected pilot within the American Airlines ranks. The flight to Washington Dulles was routine. He shared the cockpit with First Officer William Applegate and his longtime friend Stacy Bird, a Frontier Air captain riding in the jump seat to D.C. after a hunting trip in West Texas.

"Bill, Stacy and I would like to say hello to a friend in first class. Would you mind taking over for a bit?" asked Gray.

Applegate had flown right seat with Gray in the past and had earned Gray's confidence.

"Absolutely, fellows, go ahead. She's flyin' herself anyway," said Applegate.

Gray and Bird unbuckled their harnesses and took a quick glance at the controls to confirm everything was in order. He and Bird slipped into the galley through the secured cockpit door, which automatically locked behind them.

"Hi, guys," said Karen Mosely, the chief flight attendant. "May I get you boys anything?"

"I don't think so, Karen, but thanks," said Gray. "We're gonna holler at 3B for a minute before we descend into Dulles."

Captains Gray and Bird strolled down the aisle behind her to greet a former Air Force buddy—when the aircraft took a sudden lurch upward. Gray grabbed the headrests of the seats on both sides of the aisle and ducked to look out the windows for a cause—clear blue skies. The plane quickly corrected, steadying for a moment before nosing downward into a steep descent. Gasps and screams erupted throughout the cabin.

"Is your FO okay?" asked Bird.

Gray knew what he meant by this question. Since the mysterious disappearance of Malaysia Flight 370 and the deliberate crash of Germanwings Flight 9525, every pilot looked at the members of their crew with a different set of eyes. He locked eyes with Bird, both of them sharing the same thought. If they'd hit turbulence, why didn't Applegate activate the Fasten Seat Belt signs?

"Back to the cockpit," he said, edging brusquely by Captain Bird.

Gray reached the intercom console next to the cockpit access door and pressed the pound key, praying for Applegate to respond.

CHAPTER 2

May 8, 2016
3:07 p.m.
The Hack House
Binney Street
East Cambridge, Massachusetts

Andrew Lau stared intently at the iMac monitor array as Leonid
Malvalaha deftly navigated the mouse. Malvalaha and Lau's other
longtime graduate assistant, Anna Fakhri, had continued in their new
endeavor, despite the potential risk of criminal prosecution.

Through the process of pen testing, Lau identified zero-day
vulnerabilities in a computer network and took advantage of the
security holes before the network's IT department could find a
solution. Once the vulnerability window was identified, the zero-day
attack inserted malware into the system. The *Game*, as Lau called it,
required the attacked entity to pay a ransom in exchange for a patch
to their security. Prior to today, their hacks didn't directly risk lives,
though their February hack on behalf of the Las Vegas service
employees union resulted in many unforeseen deaths. They were
more selective in their project after Las Vegas, until now.

"Malvalaha, run us through the hack," said Lau, patting his trusted
associate on the shoulder as he walked by.

Lau's core group consisted of Malvalaha, Fakhri and newcomer
Herm Walthaus, who had proven himself by creating a cascading
blackout of the Las Vegas power grid—no small feat. In a way, this
was a team of misfits—although talented ones. They came from
diverse backgrounds but shared a common goal of advancing their
personal wealth.

"We're monitoring American Airlines Flight 129, which departed Dallas around forty-five minutes ago," stated Malvalaha.

His desk resembled the cockpit of a sophisticated aircraft, with six flat-panel monitors at his disposal. He pointed to the screen that displayed FlightAware, an online tool providing up-to-the-second statistics on any airline flight.

"Flight 129 is currently over St. Louis and has adjusted its flight path directly to Washington Dulles airport. The aircraft is a Boeing 757-200, flying at approximately four hundred eighty knots, or five hundred and fifty miles per hour. Altitude thirty-three thousand feet."

"Tell us what your research has shown," said Lau.

Fakhri addressed her former professor, now hacking partner. "Since 9/11, there have been conspiracy theories surrounding the commandeering of the four aircraft by the terrorists," said Fakhri. "One such theory is the aircraft was part of a false-flag attack initiated by the government. As the argument goes, based upon 2001 technology, NORAD—the North American Aerospace Defense Command—took control of the planes and purposefully crashed them into the World Trade Center and the Pentagon. The most prevalent reason cited for the false-flag operation is that the government wanted to justify initiating a war in the Middle East."

"For our purposes, we're not interested in the false-flag theories," said Malvalaha. "We focused on the concept of the remote takeover of a commercial aircraft. The technology exists, and it has, in fact, been used by the military in the past. Today, we will hack the aircraft via the flight management system, *and* make ourselves known."

"My father is a pilot for the 757-200 airframe," said Walthaus. "We always had sophisticated flight simulators in our home growing up, and naturally they provided more entertainment for me than a PlayStation. I've never physically flown an aircraft, but I am an expert on the flight sim."

"I thought the FAA disproved the theories surrounding remote access of the onboard computers," said Lau.

"True to an extent," said Fakhri. "A security consultant from

Germany claimed to have hacked an aircraft using an Android telephone application. Later, one of his peers accessed the aircraft's network by connecting through the in-flight entertainment system. He then used a modified version of Vortex software to compromise the cockpit's system."

"When pressed for a response, the FAA was selective in its choice of words," said Malvalaha. "They equivocated using the phrases *described technique* and *using the technology the consultant has claimed*."

Lau laughed after this statement.

"The government has a lot of experience with misdirection," said Lau. "Our most sophisticated operations were panned as impossible by the experts and their friends in the media—even after we successfully accomplished them!"

"When researching this online, we discovered that American Airlines and Boeing launched a Bug Bounty program, offering a million free air-miles to the good guys—the white-hat hackers," said Walthaus. "These *ethical and conscientious* hackers shared their findings online. We took their findings as a starting point and found the vulnerability window we were looking for."

"Continue," said Lau.

If Lau could publish his work, he would surely win the Carnegie Foundation award as Professor of the Year. Then again, he might be teaching second-grade math to his fellow inmates.

"We're going to use the government's safeguard technology against them in two steps," said Malvalaha.

Lau turned his Red Sox cap backward—an unconscious signal that it was time to go to work.

"First, we access the Boeing Uninterruptible Autopilot system," said Fakhri. "The patent for the system was granted to Boeing in 2006, as a method of taking control of a commercial aircraft away from the pilot or flight crew in the event of a hijacking. The uninterruptible autopilot can be initiated by the pilots via onboard sensors or remotely through government satellite links."

"As far as the public knows, no Boeing aircraft has been retrofitted to include this technology, although rumors abound to the contrary," said Walthaus. "After the disappearance of Malaysia Flight 370, the Prime Minister of Malaysia claimed Boeing or *individual government agencies* utilized the uninterruptible autopilot to down the aircraft. I'm sure he alluded to the CIA."

"An online search supported his theory," said Fakhri. "We researched the rules issued by the FAA on the Federal Register website and found a Special Condition granted to Boeing for the Model 777 aircraft, allowing the installation of the uninterruptible autopilot software."

"But we're tracking a 757," said Lau.

"Yes, we are," said Walthaus. "The FAA, in its action, authorized Boeing to conduct tests of the new system in six of its 757 aircraft, plus the system was initially designed for the 757. We researched all of the top contractors who work under Boeing's Defense division. Typically, new technology ends up in the hands of our Defense Department."

"We found the company hired to install the system—Alion Science and Technology," said Fakhri. "Their technology solutions sector manager, Robert Hurt, gave a presentation at a Raytheon trade show last year, which was published online. After some digging, we have the details on the six 757 aircraft participating in the program."

"American Airlines Flight 129 is one of them," said Malvalaha.

CHAPTER 3

May 8, 2016
3:12 p.m.
American Airlines Flight 129
33,000 Feet
Near Evansville, Indiana

Gray exhaled deeply when the green light on the keypad illuminated. He and Bird quickly entered the cockpit and slammed the door shut.

"What the hell is going on, Bill!" exclaimed Gray as he climbed into his seat and strapped in. Bird positioned himself in the jump seat. Gray quickly examined the onboard computer monitor and activated the Fasten Seat Belt sign.

"Talk to me, Billy!"

"The controls are unresponsive," muttered Applegate. "We are in a rapid descent, and the controls will not respond to any of my commands."

"You have to call a Mayday, Randy," said Bird.

Gray looked at the altitude control indicator. They were in a descent, but not an insurmountable one—yet. The altimeter read twenty-four thousand feet.

"Billy, are you with me?" asked Gray.

Applegate barely muttered a response.

"Billy, why don't you trade seats with Captain Bird," said Gray. "You need a break, and Stacy is an experienced captain. Come on now, let Stacy swap with you."

Applegate slowly removed his seat harness and traded seats with Bird, who immediately leaned across the center console.

"Should I escort him off the flight deck?" asked Bird.

"He's just shook up," said Gray. "Call in the Mayday, and let me figure this out."

Bird's attempt to access the onboard computer proved fruitless. The keyboard was unresponsive.

"We're one hundred miles east of St. Louis," said Gray. "Try SDF. Wait, not Louisville. We'll need Indianapolis Center."

"Mayday, Mayday, Mayday, Indianapolis Center. American Airlines one-two-niner heavy declaring an emergency," said Bird. "I say again. Mayday, Mayday, Mayday, Indianapolis ZID. American Airlines one-two-niner heavy declaring an emergency."

"American one-two-niner, this is Indianapolis Center. We copy your Mayday," said a representative of the Indianapolis Air Route Traffic Control Center. The primary responsibility of Indianapolis Center was to monitor and separate flights within the seventy-three thousand square miles it covered in the Midwest. Today, a new task presented itself. "What is the nature of your emergency?"

"Indianapolis Center, onboard controls are unresponsive. We are under power and in a steady descent now passing twenty-two thousand feet," said Bird. "All other flight deck functions appear normal."

"Roger, American one-two-niner. All stations. All stations. Indianapolis Center. Mayday situation in progress. Stop transmitting. Repeat. Mayday situation in progress. Stop all transmissions."

Gray sat back in the pilot's seat and looked around the Orbiter flight deck, searching for clues—and answers. Nothing made sense. The entire console appeared normal. The monitors functioned properly, displaying their current flight parameters; however, the keyboard for the onboard computer continued to be unresponsive.

"We're leveling off," said Bird, pointing at the altitude control indicator. "Son of a bitch, we're holding steady at twenty K. I've never seen anything like this."

Neither had Gray.

"American one-two-niner, this is Indianapolis Center. Boeing technical team is en route, and Homeland Security has been notified."

"Roger, Indianapolis Center," said Bird. "Be advised, altitude has leveled off at twenty thousand feet. Steady on original course."

"American one-two-niner. Indianapolis Center. Roger."

"Homeland Security?" asked Bird.

Gray understood the gravity of their situation. If he couldn't demonstrate positive control of the aircraft, it would not be allowed to reach Washington.

CHAPTER 4

May 8, 2016
3:13 p.m.
The Hack House
Binney Street
East Cambridge, Massachusetts

"Now that we've entered the plane's Wi-Fi system, it's necessary to hack through the firewall of the aircraft communications addressing and reporting system, or ACARS," said Malvalaha. "This will give us access to the plane's onboard computer system and the uploaded flight management system data."

Lau watched intently as his protégé navigated through the plane's servers.

"You're in!" exclaimed Walthaus. "My turn, Leo."

Malvalaha relinquished his chair to Walthaus, whose only experience with an airplane was playing on his father's computer as a teen.

"The aircraft is flying on autopilot," said Fakhri. "That's good. Right about now, the pilots are relaxed and completely unaware of our presence."

"First, I will initiate the uninterruptible autopilot system, which will prevent the flight crew from interfering with us," said Walthaus. "These controls are considered *fly-by-wire,* which have replaced the conventional manual controls of the aircraft with an electronic interface. The yokes that control the aircraft may provide certain inputs into a flight-control system, but with the uninterruptible autopilot system initiated, the crew can flail around all they want, and their actions will not be recognized.

"First, we'll adjust the altitude to twenty-six thousand feet—just to let them know we're flying their plane," he continued. "Watch here."

Walthaus pointed to FlightAware, and Lau turned his attention to the screen. When Walthaus refreshed the screen, the airspeed had declined, along with the aircraft's altitude.

"Whoa!" exclaimed Walthaus. "Sorry about that! It's hard to adjust the controls using a mouse and its cursor. I just took the plane into a dive and probably scared the shit out of everybody on board. Let me level this off at twenty thousand feet."

"Is that too low?" asked Lau.

"No, eighteen thousand feet is considered the upper end of an air traffic's transitional level, where the most activity takes place," said Walthaus. "We'll maintain this altitude and course for a few minutes, to give everyone on board an opportunity to catch their breath. Then we'll climb back to thirty-three thousand feet."

Ordinarily, the Zero Day Gamers had a profit motive. The hijack by hacking of the American Airlines flight was a test. Today, they would determine whether the hack could be achieved, in addition to gauging the government's response.

"At this point, the pilots have probably reported a Mayday to the nearest air traffic control tower—either St. Louis or Louisville," said Malvalaha. "Their flight training would dictate a simple procedure of turning off the autopilot and resuming control of the aircraft manually. Unfortunately for them, the Boeing Uninterruptible Autopilot system has built-in safeguards that prevent the pilots from overriding our controls."

"What prevents NORAD or the FAA from taking over the operation of the plane via its satellite controls?" asked Lau.

"We've installed a version of the TeslaCrypt Ransomware onto the plane's servers," said Malvalaha. "This malware blocks access to the aircraft's onboard computers by everybody until released by us. In the future, we'll provide them a message with a monetary demand. Today, we're just sending a message."

CHAPTER 5

May 8, 2016
3:17 p.m.
NORAD—Air Defense Operations Center
Cheyenne Mountain Air Force Station, Colorado

"Sir, Wright-Patterson has been notified of the situation," said the technical sergeant who was manning the console tracking American Airlines Flight 129. "I have Lieutenant Colonel Darren Reynolds on the line, sir."

Colonel Arnold pressed the remote transmit button for his headset. "Colonel Reynolds, this is Colonel James Arnold. Please stay on the line as we assess the situation."

"Colonel Arnold, we have scrambled two F-16s. Time is running out. Once ADOC was notified, we ceased communications with the Indianapolis Air Traffic Control Center and turned comms over to you."

"Thank you, Colonel," said Arnold. "Sergeant, contact the aircraft."

"American Airlines one-two-niner, United States Air Force Air Defense Operations Center. Over," said the airman.

After a moment, the response came through the overhead speakers.

"Air Defense, this is Captain Randy Gray."

"Captain Gray, this is Colonel Arnold. What steps have you taken to gain control of your aircraft?" asked Colonel Arnold.

"The most logical step is to turn off the plane's autopilot," said Gray. "But the autopilot is unresponsive. In fact, all of our controls are unresponsive. We've had no flight control for nearly seventeen minutes now."

"Stand by, Captain Gray," said Colonel Arnold.

He pointed to the sergeant to mute the conversation, waiting several seconds before addressing his team.

"If this 757 is outfitted with Boeing's new autopilot system, why haven't we simply taken control of the aircraft?"

"Malware has been inserted into the aircraft's onboard server network, preventing any type of outside access," said another airman. "Boeing technical support is working on a solution, but so far they have been unsuccessful."

"Colonel Reynolds, what is the ETA on your F-16s?" asked Colonel Arnold.

Arnold took a deep breath during the pause and studied the global positioning of Flight 129. The plane would be over a desolate area of Eastern Kentucky in roughly ten minutes. He had to escalate this to USNorthCom. He was not going to sentence 237 passengers and crew to their death without further orders.

Chapter 6

May 8, 2016
3:23 p.m.
F-16 "Fighting Falcons"
180ᵗʰ Fighter Wing
24,000 Feet
Near Lexington, Kentucky

"Roger, Giant Killer, awaiting orders," said Smash Seven, the lead F-16 pilot dispatched to intercept Flight 129. "We will maintain two four thousand at the four o'clock and eight o'clock positions."

"Copy, Smash Seven," said Smash Eleven, maintaining his position above the left rear of the 757 aircraft. "Smash Seven, switch to alternate frequency Charlie. Repeat, switch to alternate frequency Charlie."

"Go ahead, Smash Eleven."

"Are we going to shoot down a commercial airliner?" asked Smash Eleven.

"Certainly not what I had in mind when I woke up this morning," said Smash Seven. "It must be hijacked."

"Look, they're climbing. Return to primary frequency."

"Switching," said Smash Eleven.

"Giant Killer, Smash Seven. Aircraft appears to be in ascent. Repeat, aircraft is ascending. Now climbing to two four thousand," said Smash Seven. "Now two eight thousand. Please advise."

"Roger that, Smash Seven," said Giant Killer. "Maintain present heading and adjust altitude to three six thousand."

The F-16s rose in altitude to maintain a height advantage over the 757.

"Aircraft has leveled off at three three thousand. Heading has not changed," said Smash Seven. "We have bull's-eye on one-two-nine at three six thousand now. We are a half mile in trail."

CHAPTER 7

May 8, 2016
3:23 p.m.
American Airlines Flight 129
20,000 Feet
Near Lexington, Kentucky

"Those are F-16s," said Bird. "They've remained just behind us since they checked us out a few minutes ago."

Gray was aware the military would not hesitate to shoot them down if the plane was hijacked. Although their altitude had leveled, no one knew whether the plane would fly directly into the Atlantic or nose-dive into Washington. The government would not take that chance. He suddenly felt the urge to call his wife.

"I'm going to call Betty," said Gray.

At lower altitude, he might reach a cell tower. A second after pressing send on his phone, the plane began to climb. He initiated communications once again with the Indianapolis ZID.

"Indianapolis Center. American Airlines Flight one-two-niner. Aircraft has begun uncontrolled ascent," said Gray.

Bird called out the altimeter readings. "Twenty-three thousand. Twenty-six thousand. Thirty thousand."

"American Airlines one-two-niner, roger that. Are you able to gain control of your aircraft?"

"Negative." Gray was sweating profusely.

They were running out of time.

"Where are the F-16s, Stacy?"

"I don't have a visual. My guess is they're a thousand feet above and behind us," replied Bird.

"Captain Gray," interrupted the voice of the Air Force colonel, "I'm not going to sugarcoat this. You have about two minutes to gain control of your aircraft before you enter populated areas and D.C. airspace. Homeland Security has established certain protocols in this type of situation."

Gray and Bird exchanged glances. *How could this be happening? I really want to talk to my wife.*

"Colonel, I assure you that we have nothing to do with this," pleaded Gray. "There has to be a solution. This airplane is acting normally, except for the controls. It must be a malfunction. You can't shoot us down!"

"Randy, look!" exclaimed Bird, tapping the monitors for the onboard computer.

Gray immediately grabbed the controls, remembering that the autopilot was activated. He flipped the switch, and the plane responded to his touch. Flight 129 was his again!

"All stations, this is American Airlines one-two-niner. We have positive control of the flight. I say again, we have positive control of the flight!" said Gray.

As he and Captain Bird exchanged relieved looks, the monitor display changed:

Thank you for flying with Zero Day Gamers Airways.

APPENDIX B

PREPAREDNESS CHECKLIST
Provided by www.FreedomPreppers.com

Visit:

freedompreppers.com/preppers-checklist-net.pdf

to download your free preppers PDF print-out